Carrie Osburn Designs Presents

Doodledala 3

By Carrie Osburn

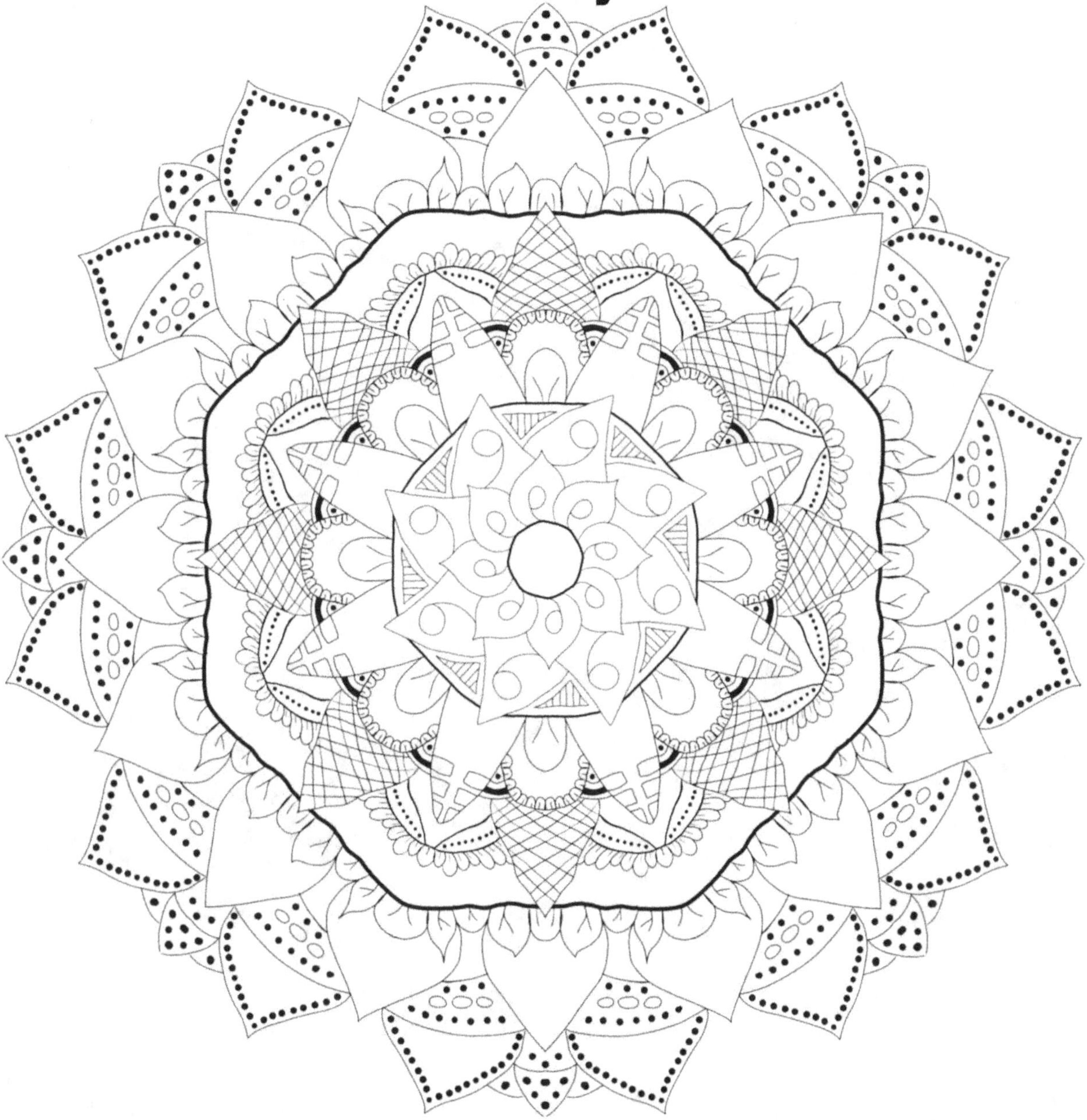

A very special thank you to Jane Adam for coloring my cover
Mandala, You did so beautifully!

Copyright

Dedication

This book is dedicated to my constant followers. Renata, Cindy, Sheryl, Eric and Chanda, Leigh. Amy Mom, and Carol. Your likes, thumbs, hearts, and comments are what keeps me going.

Thank you.
I appreciate you.

Social Media

https://carrieosburndesigns.com
facebook.com/carrieosburndesigns
https://www.etsy.com/shop/CarrieOsburnDesigns

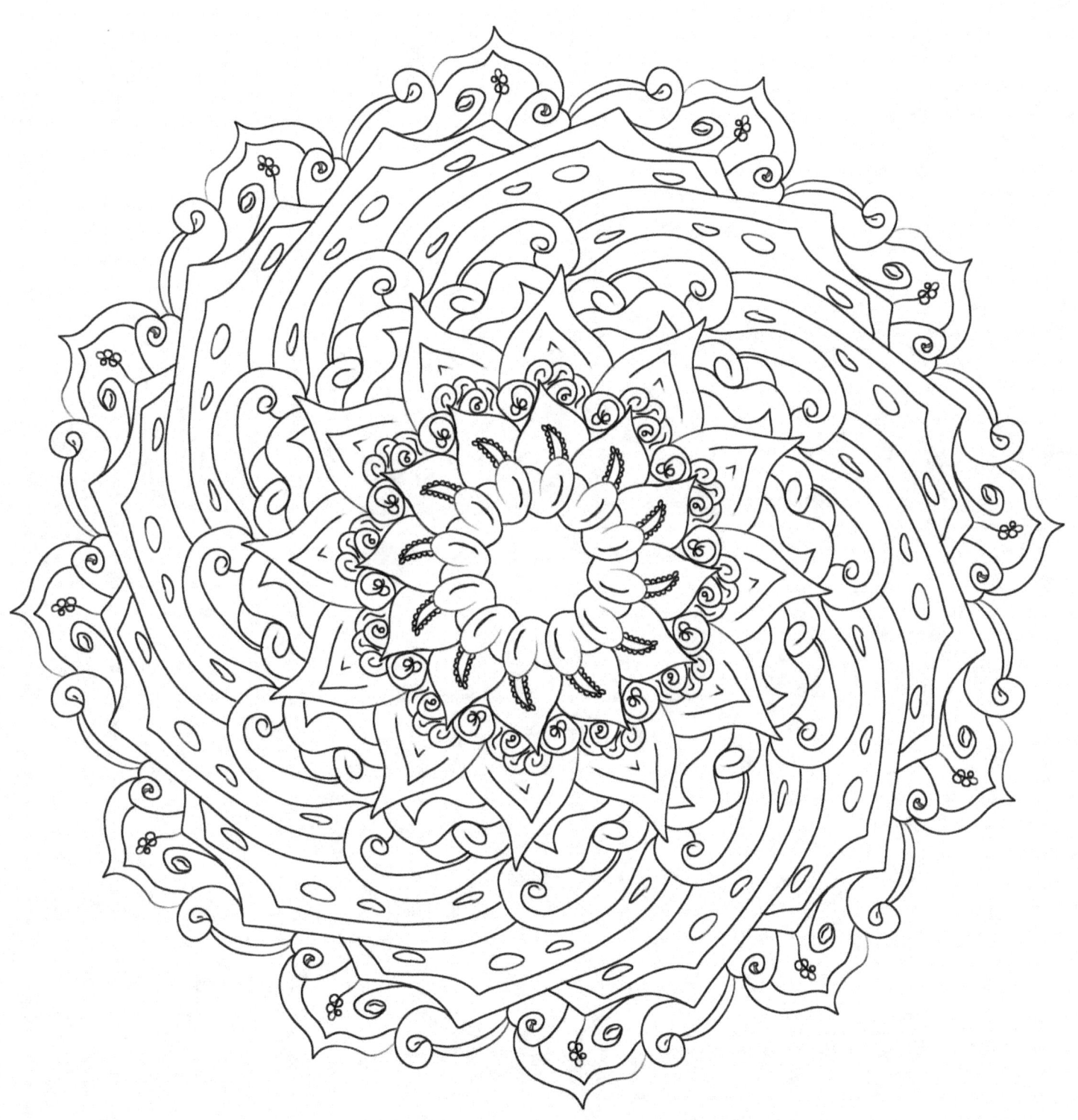

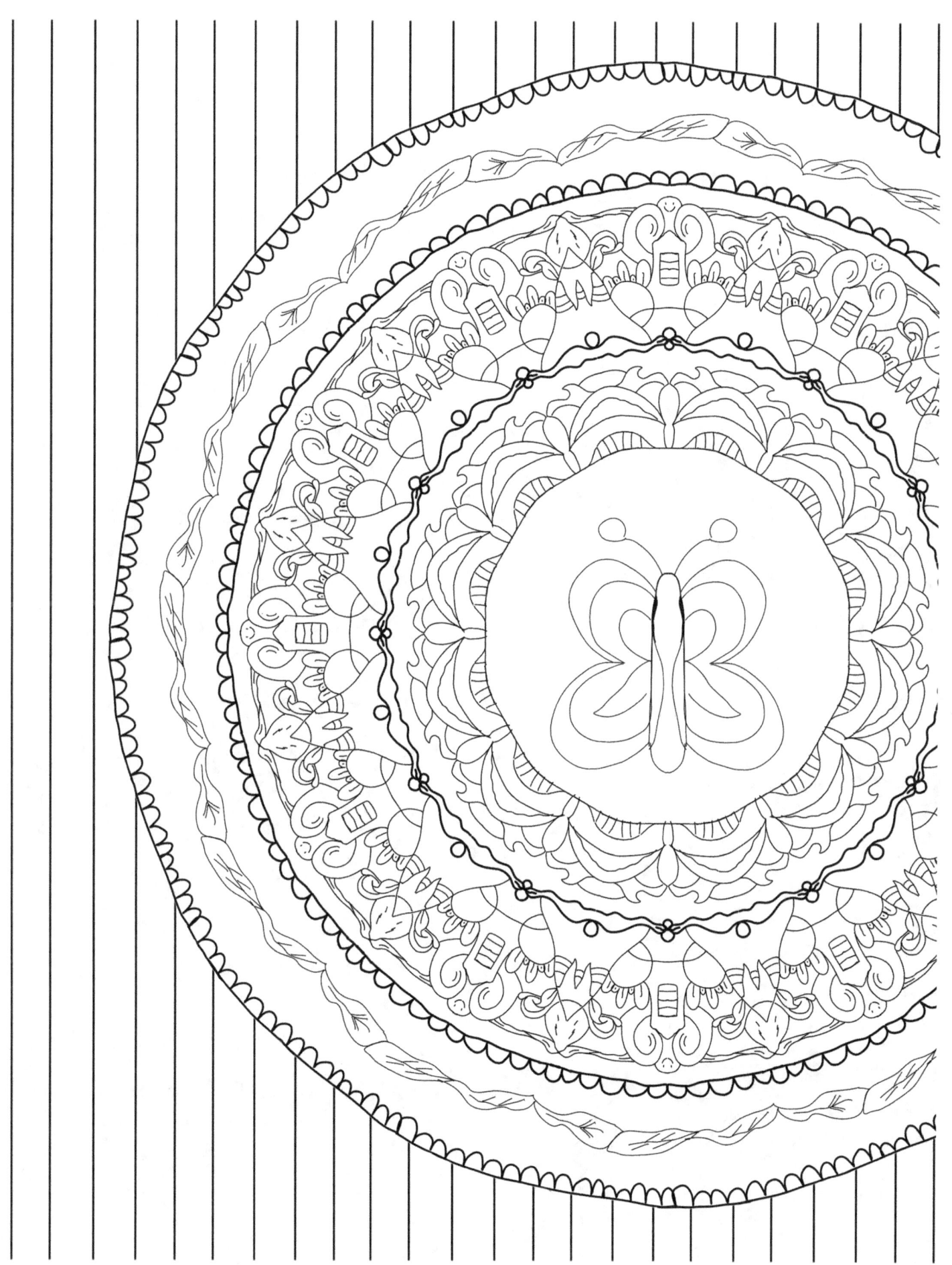

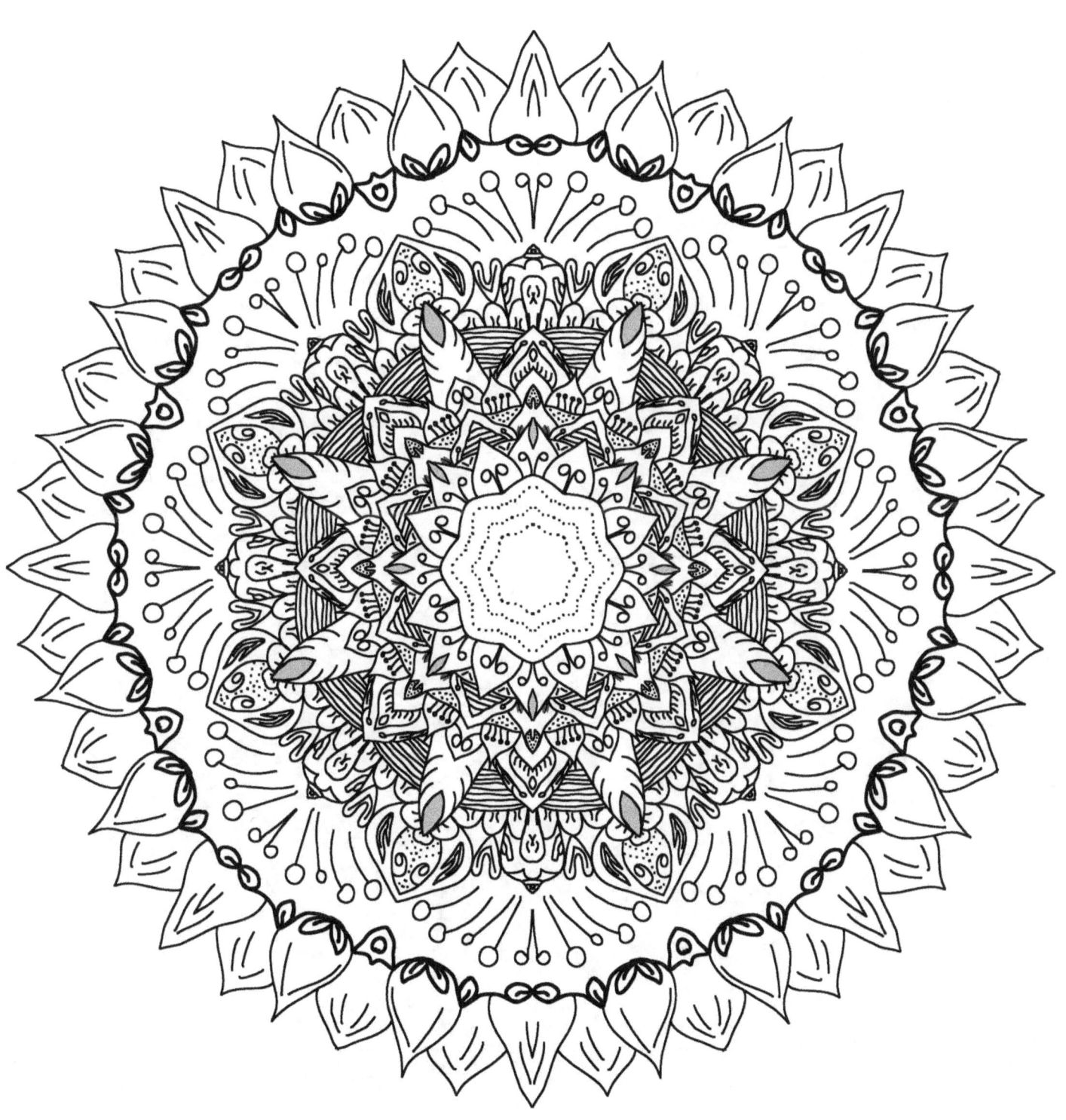

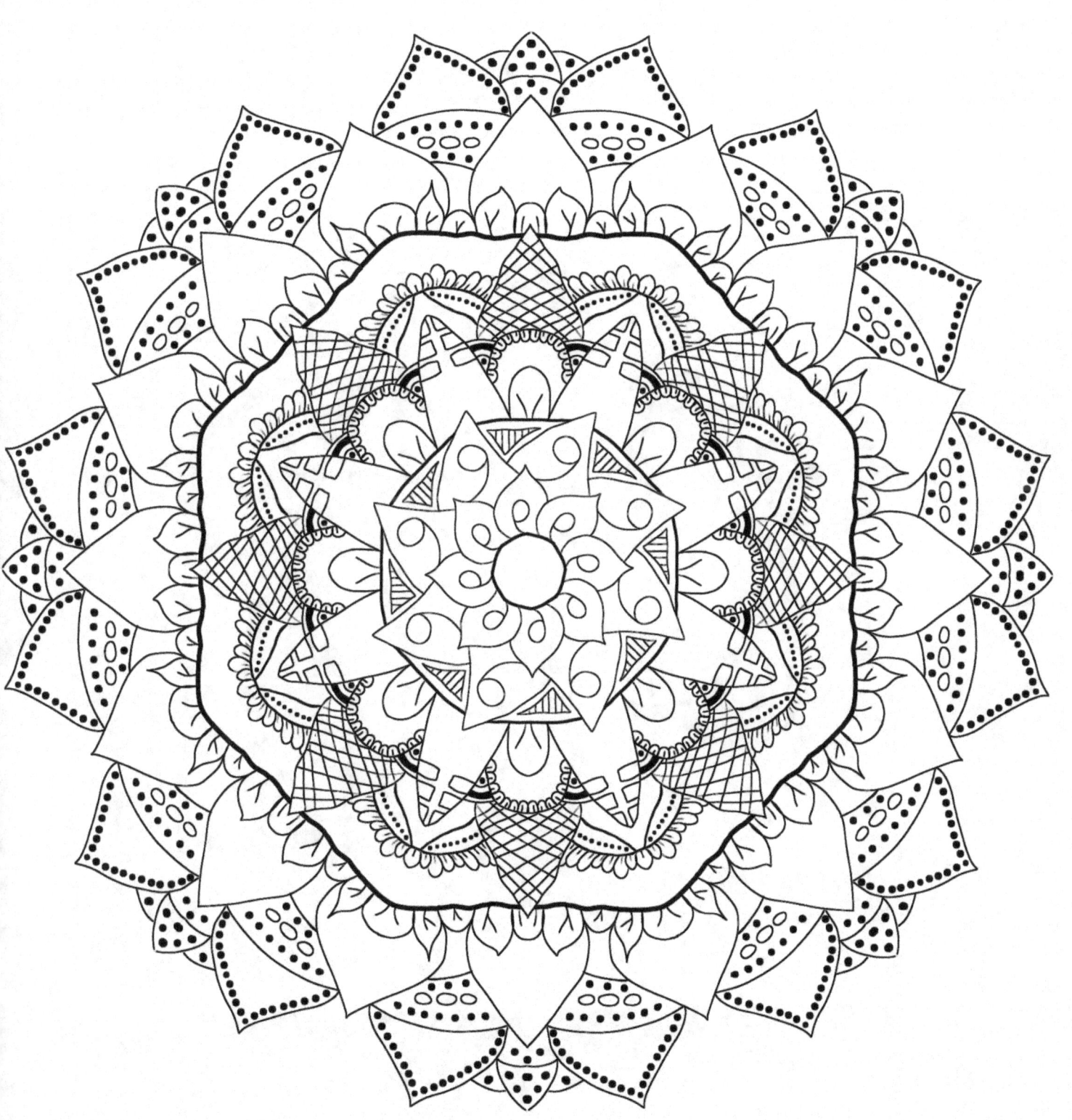

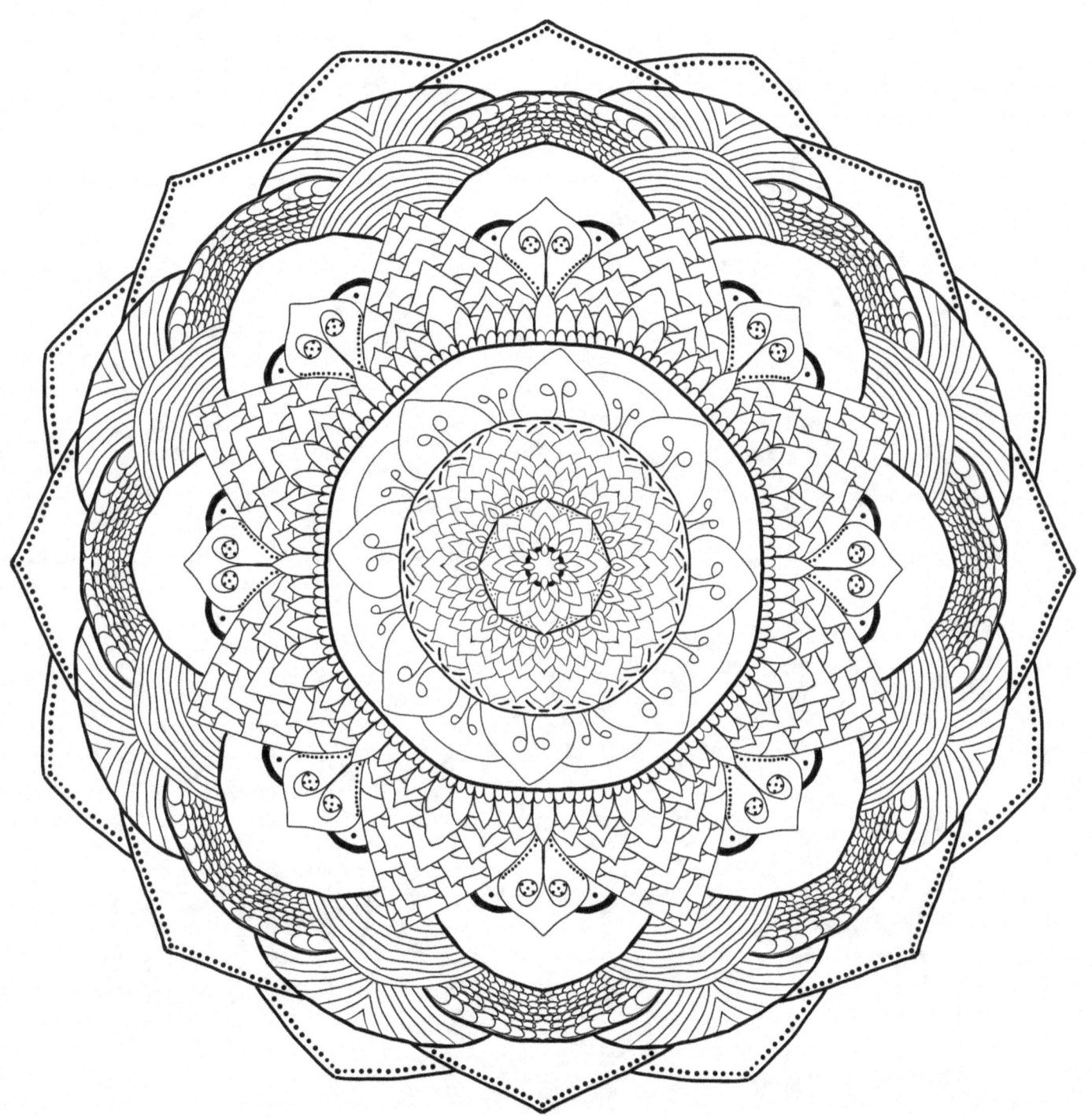

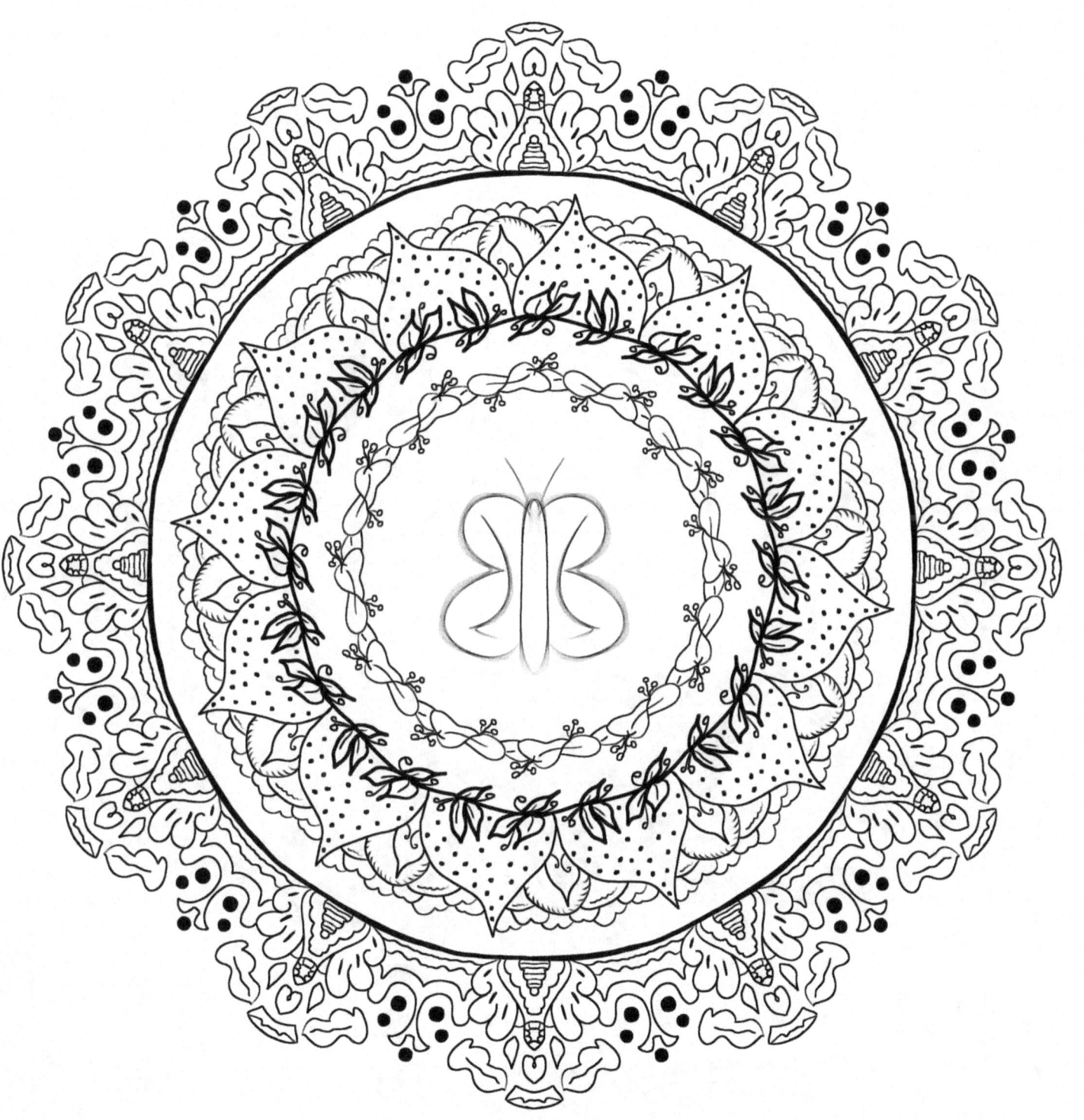

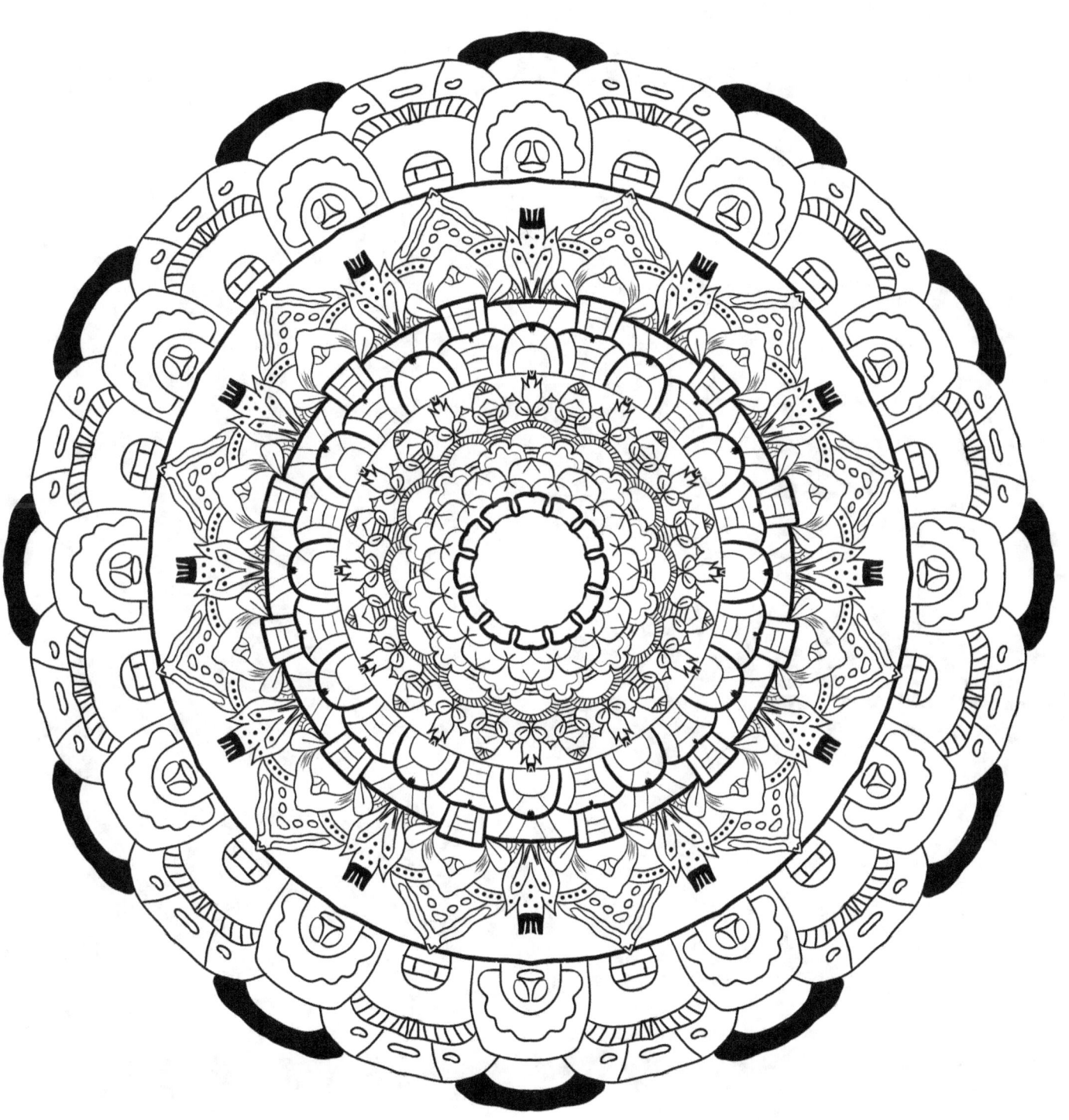

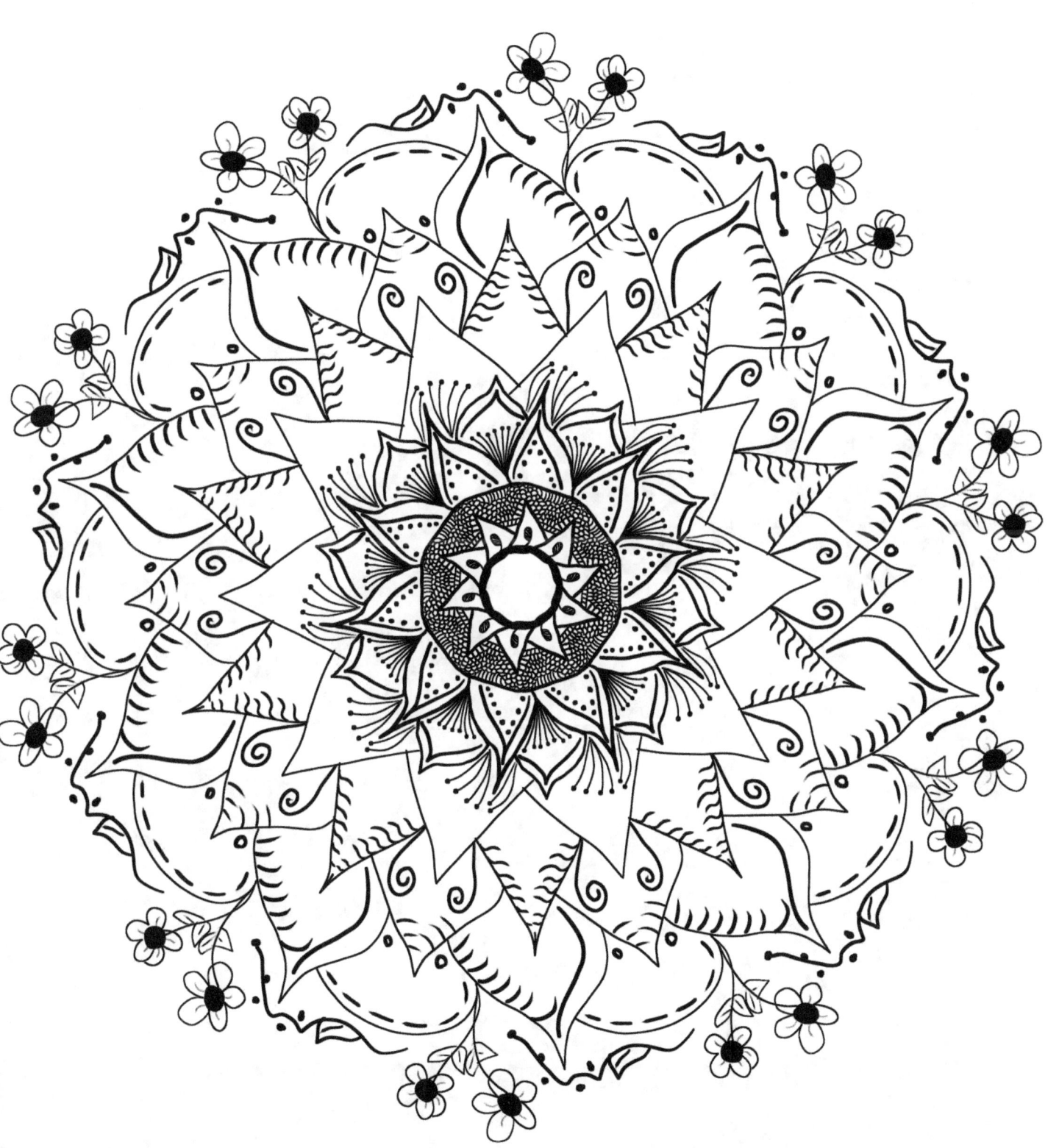

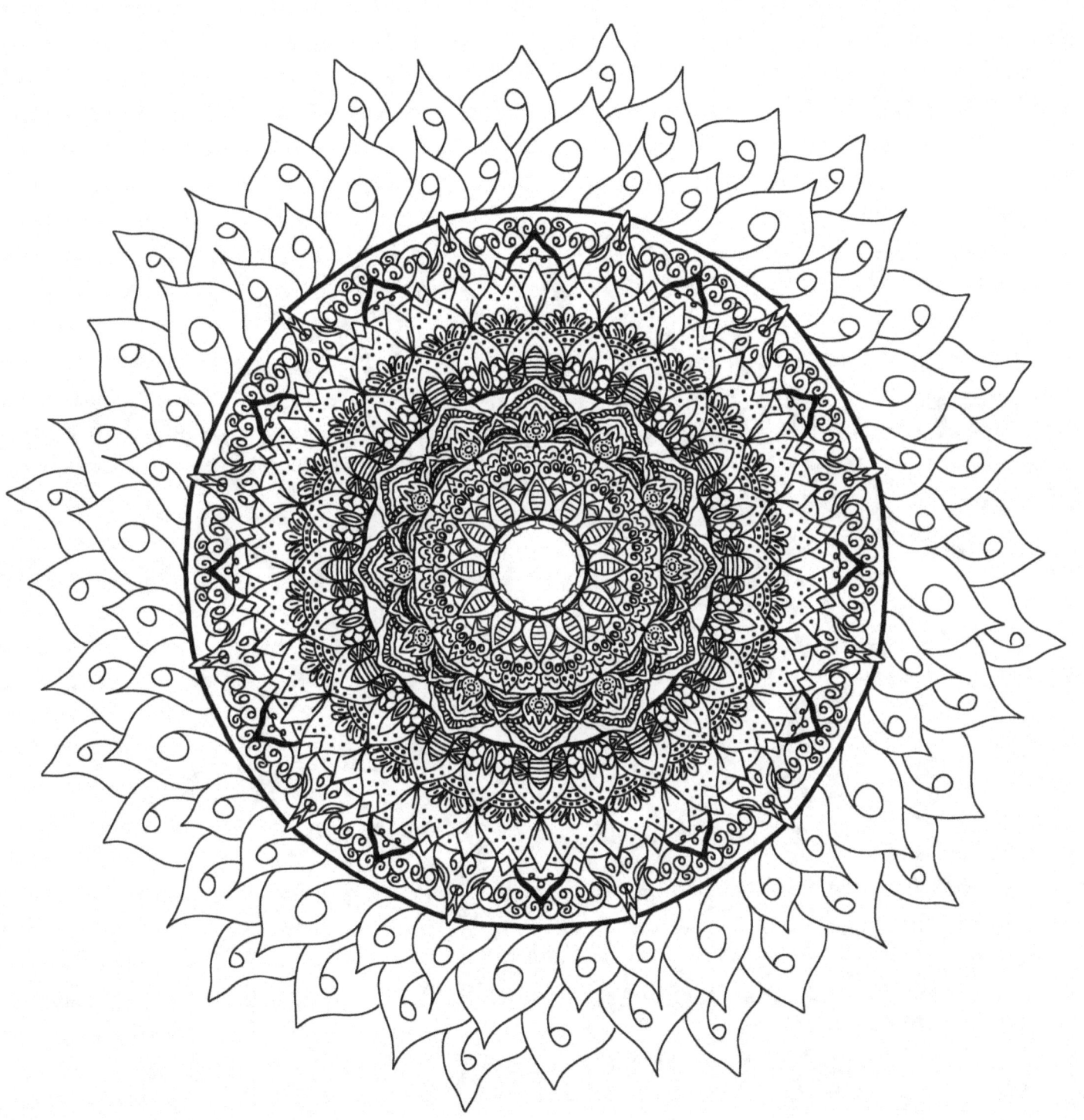

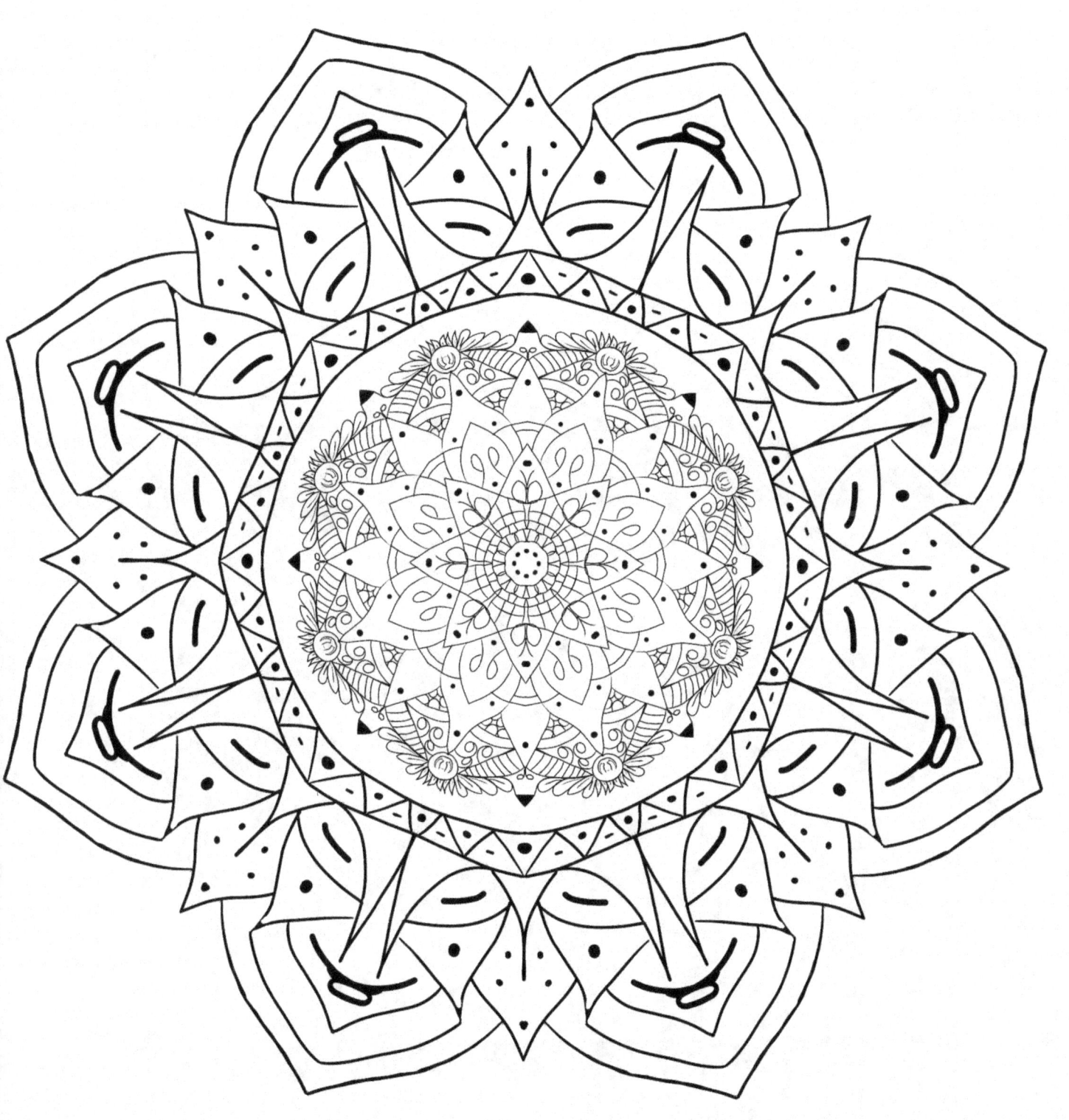

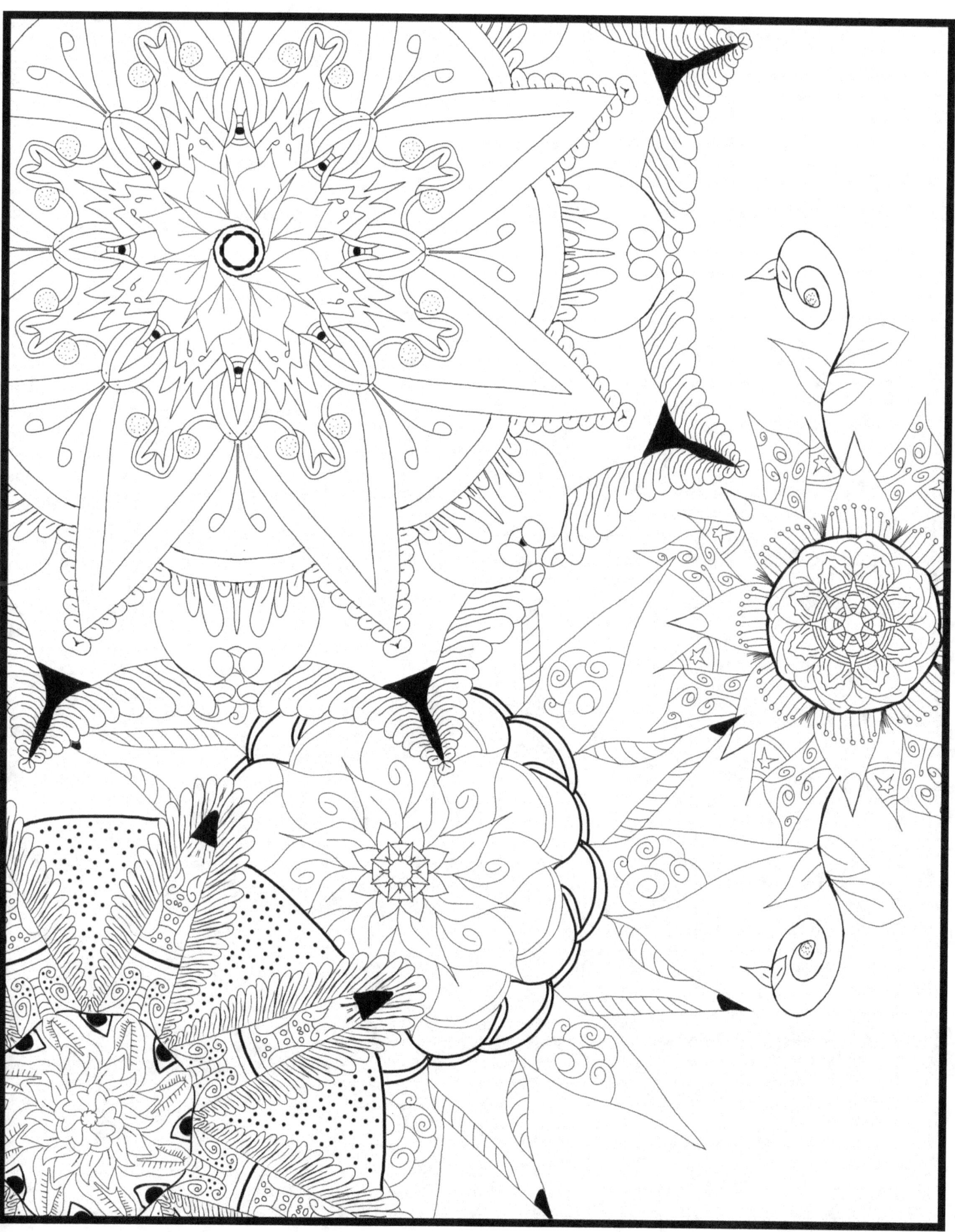

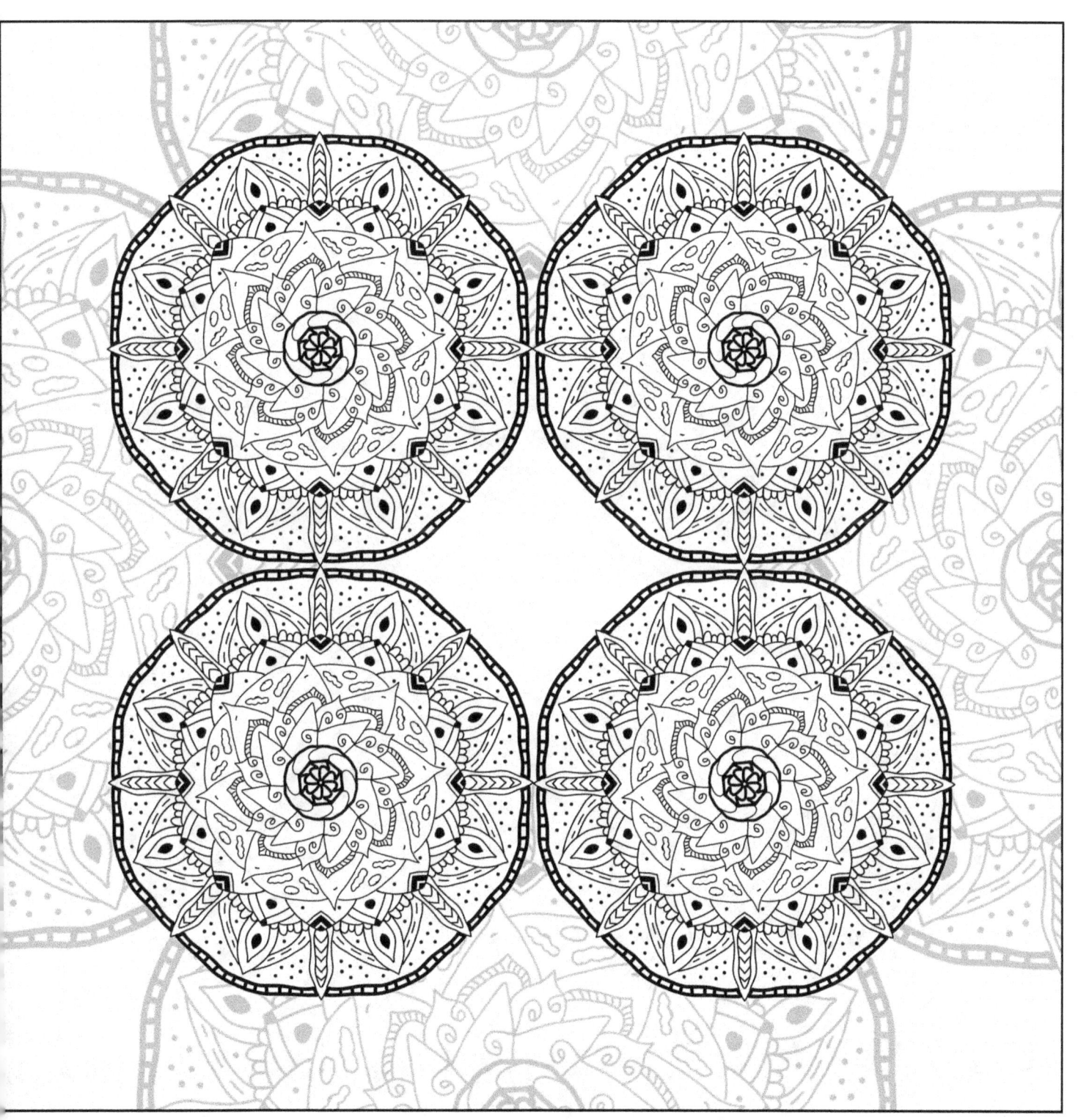

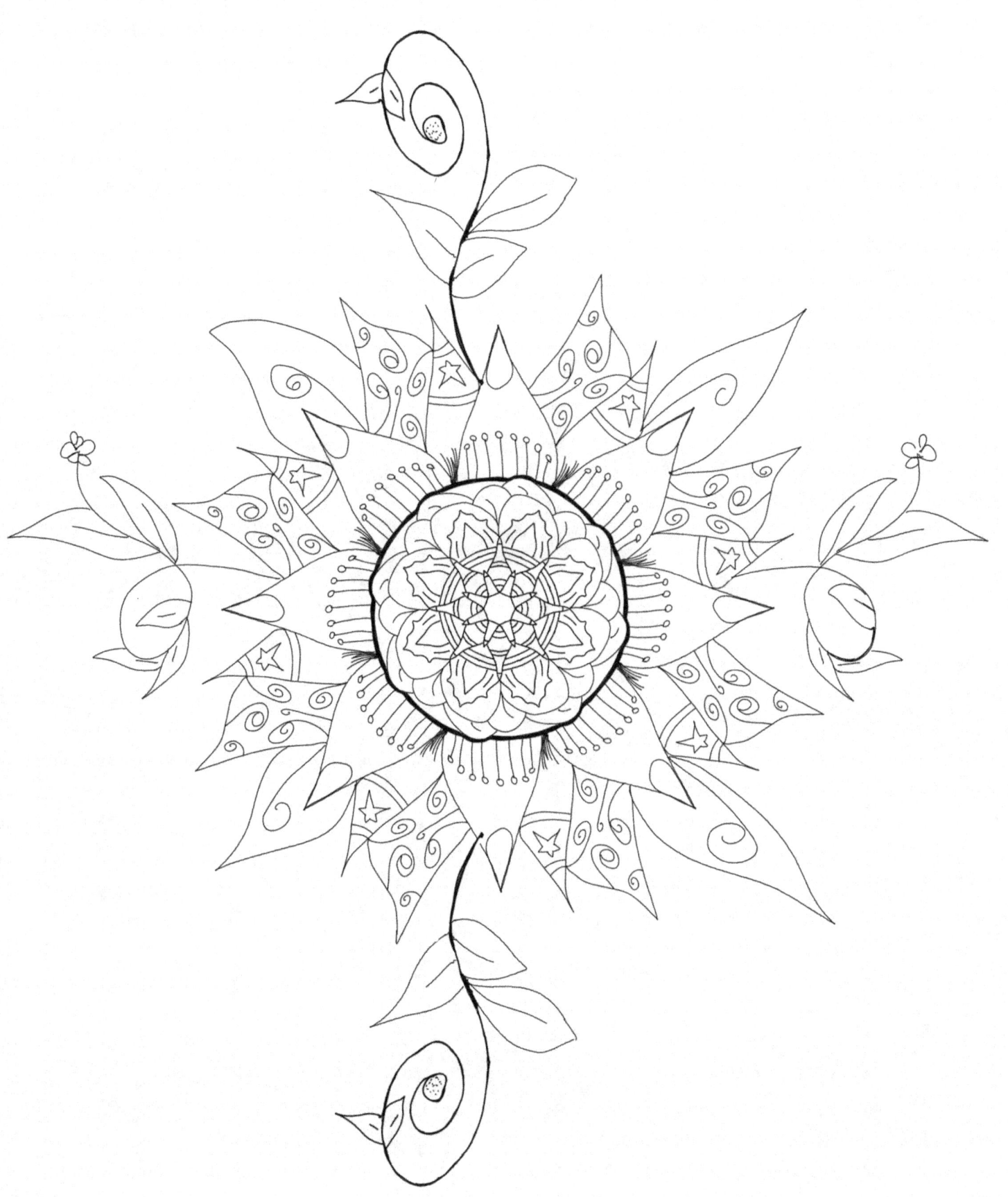

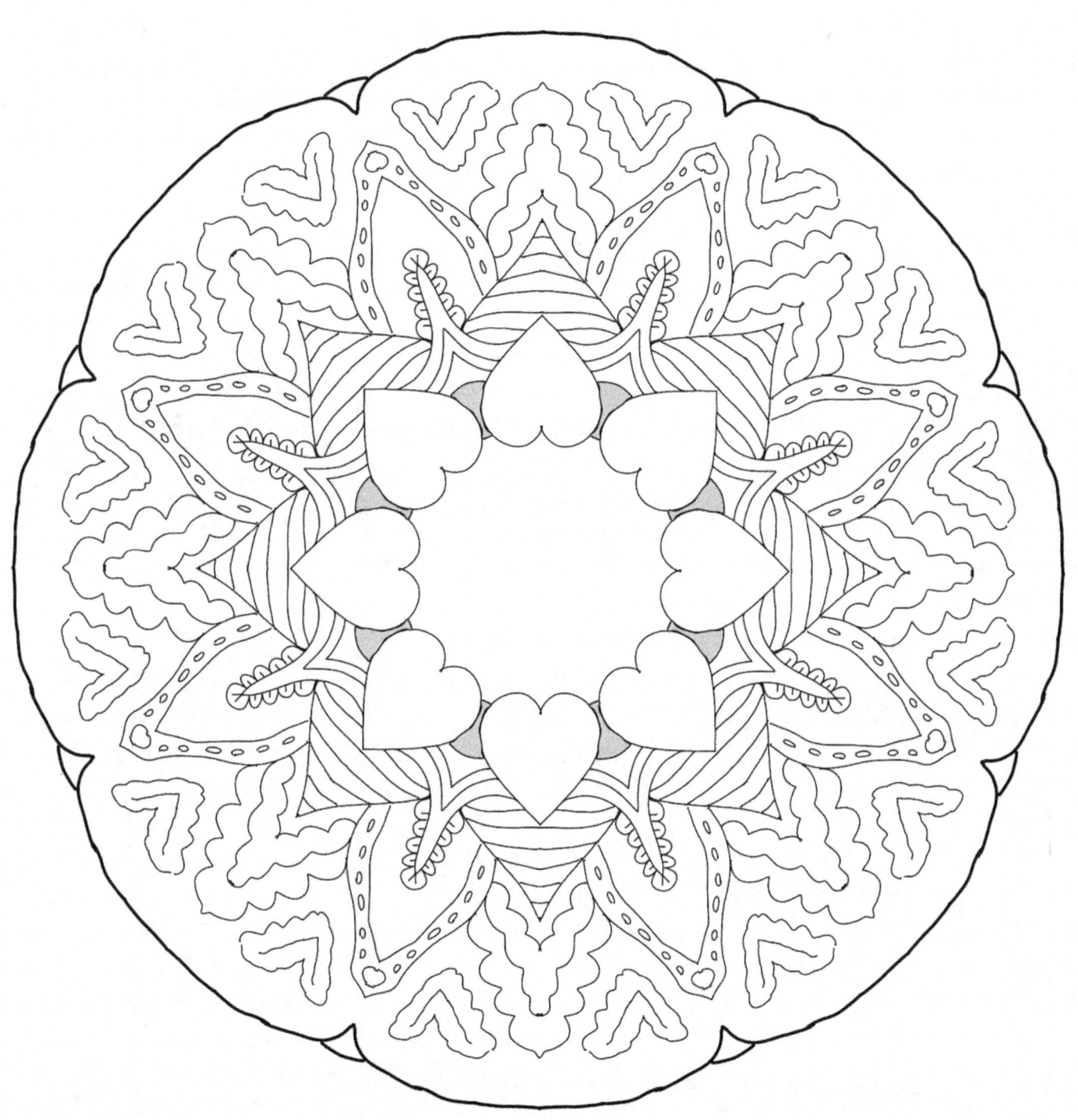

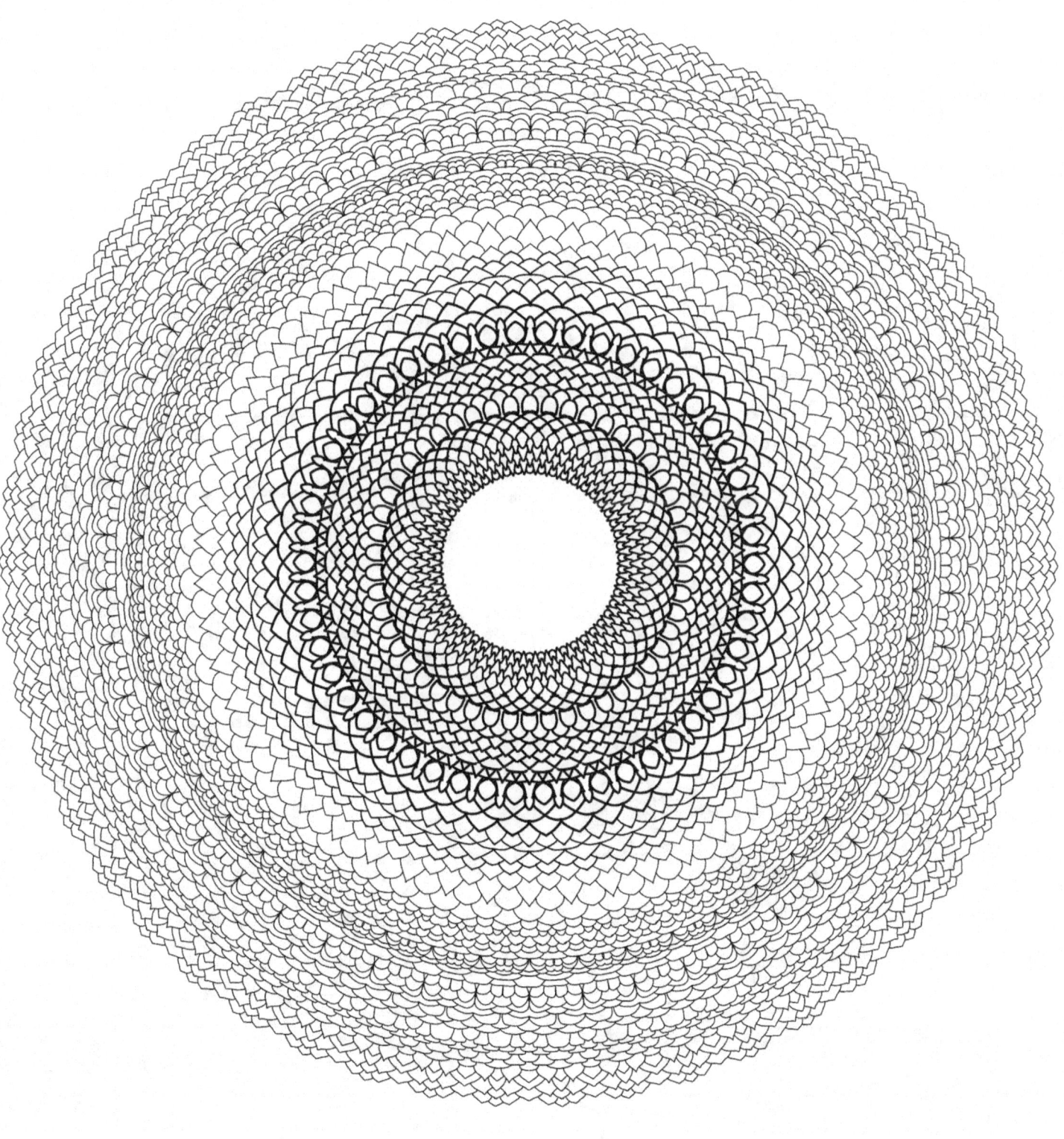

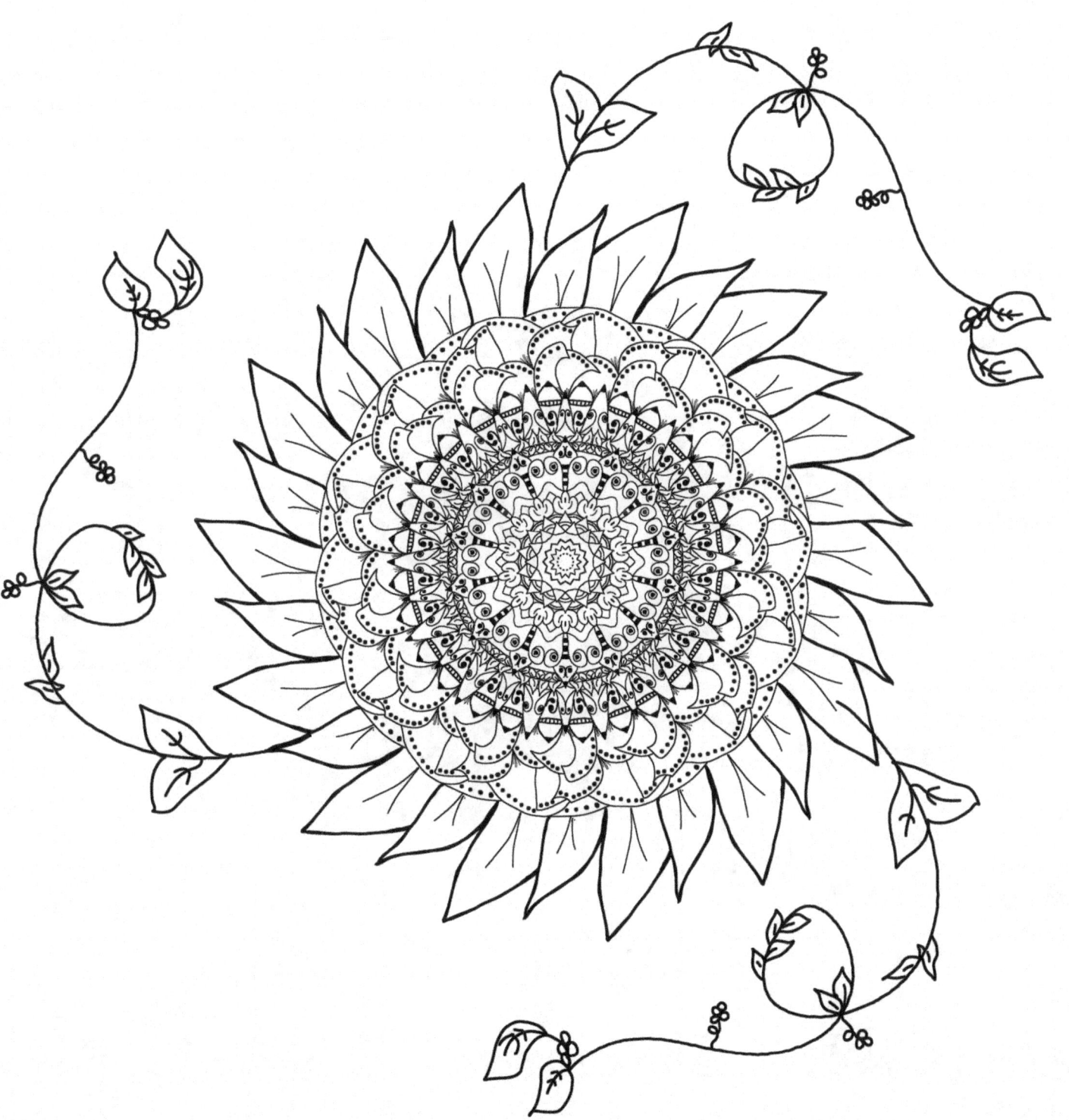

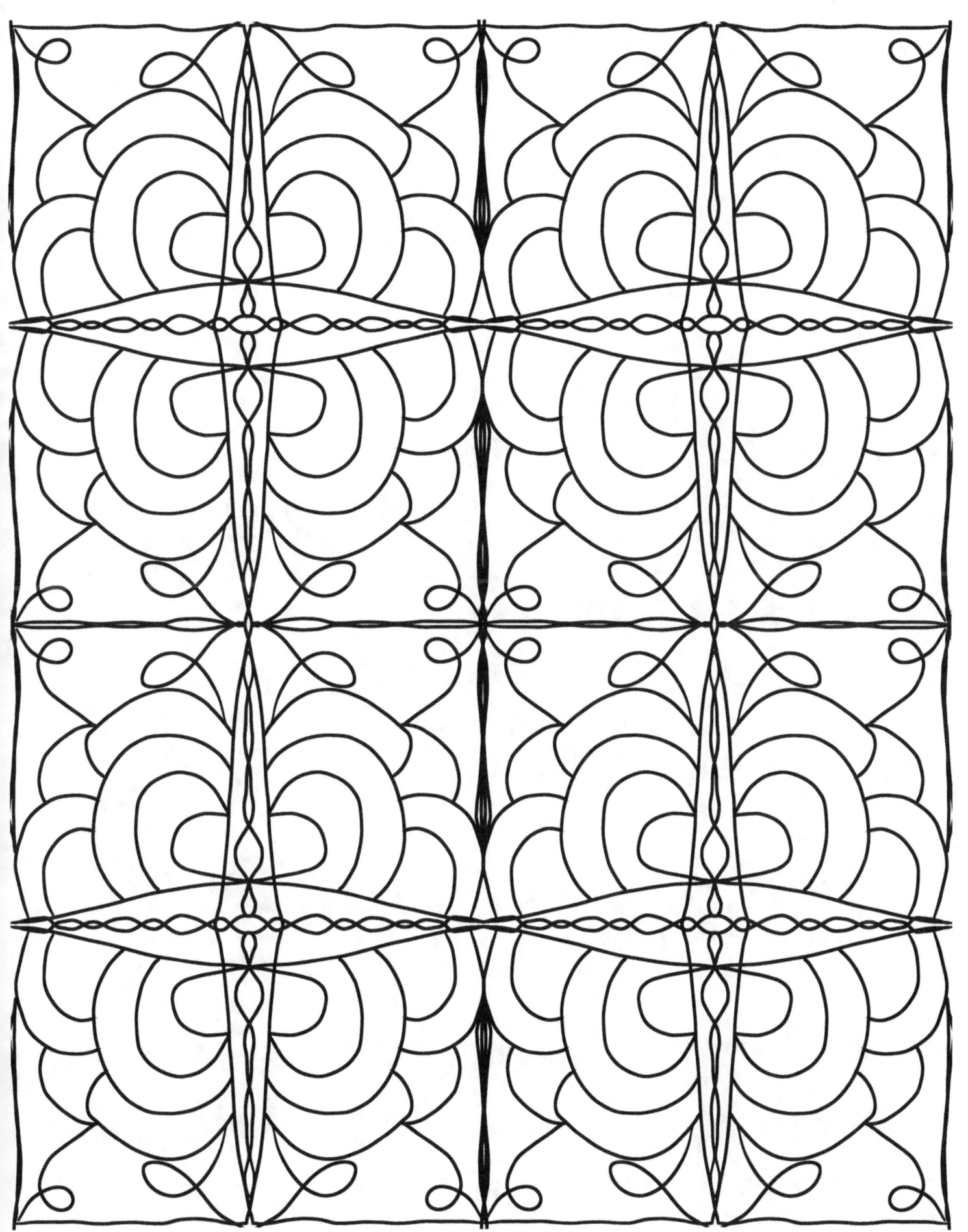

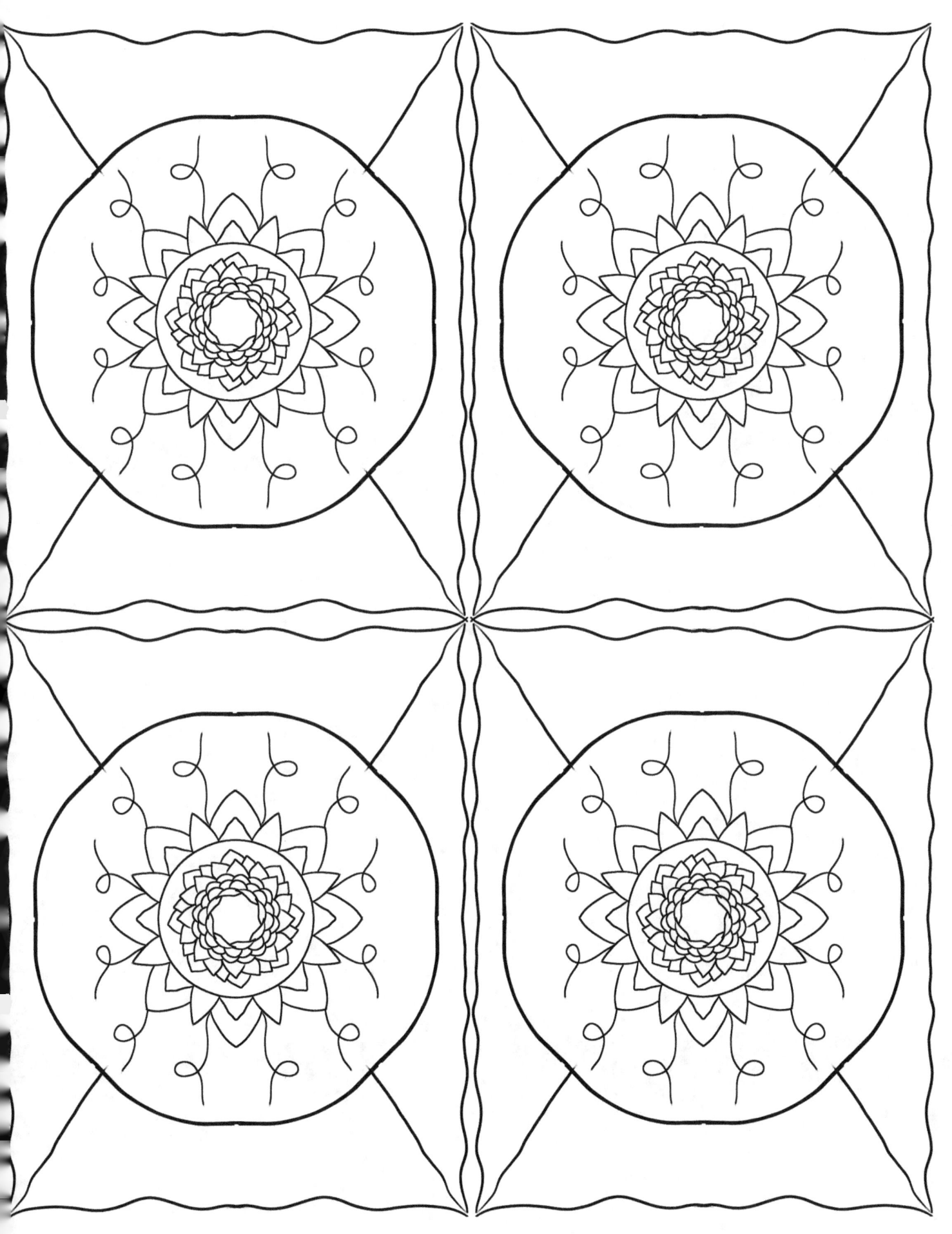

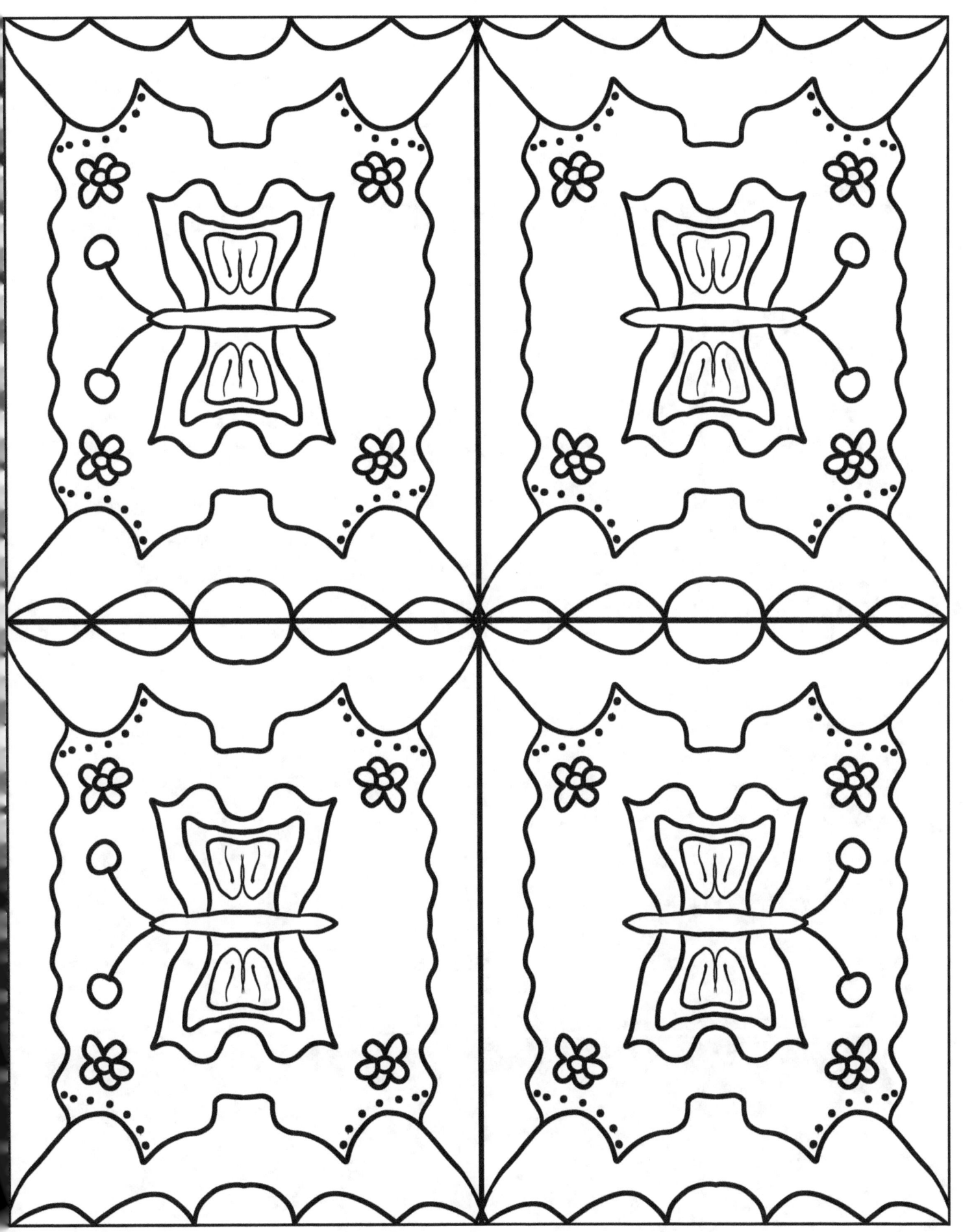

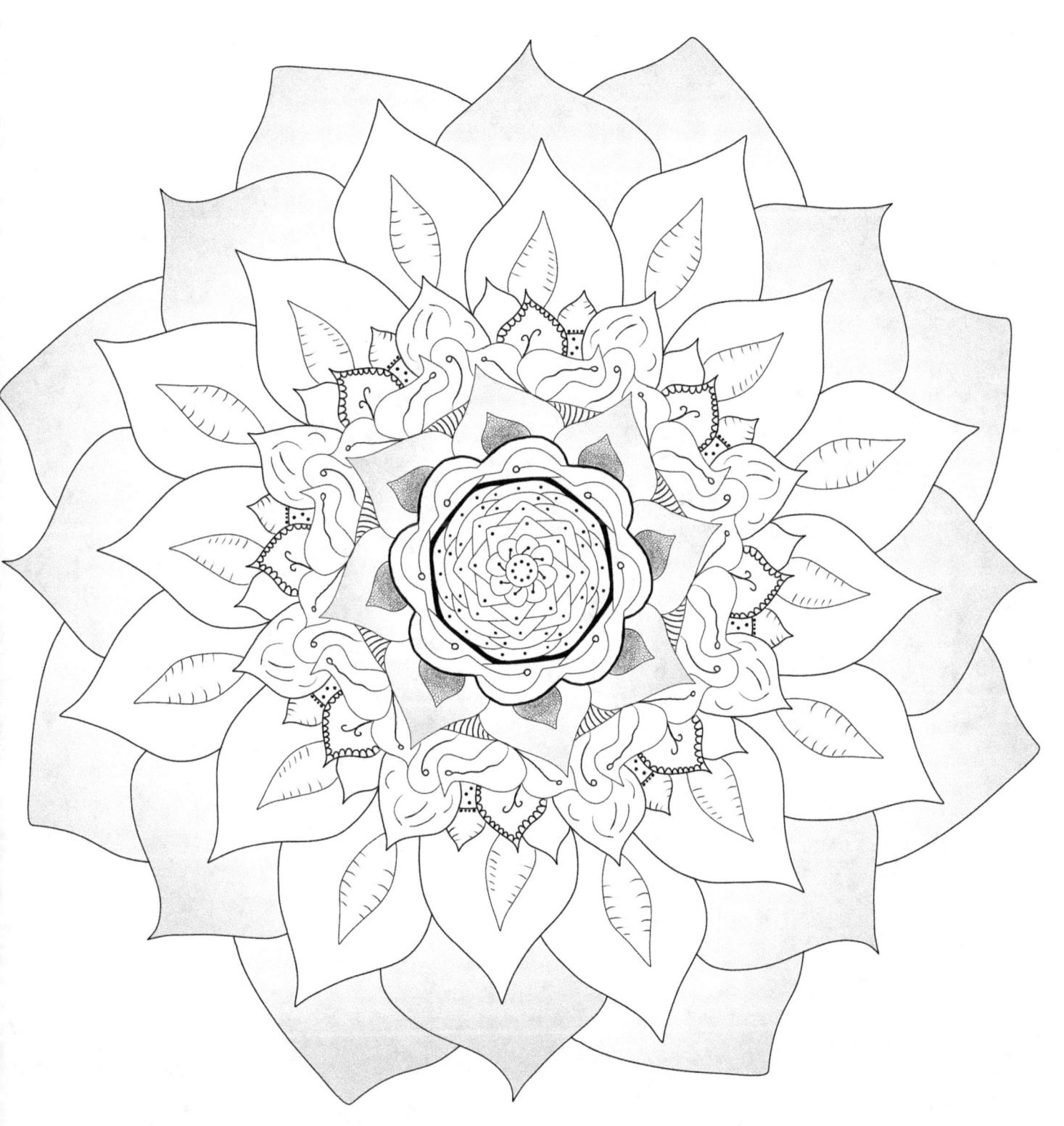

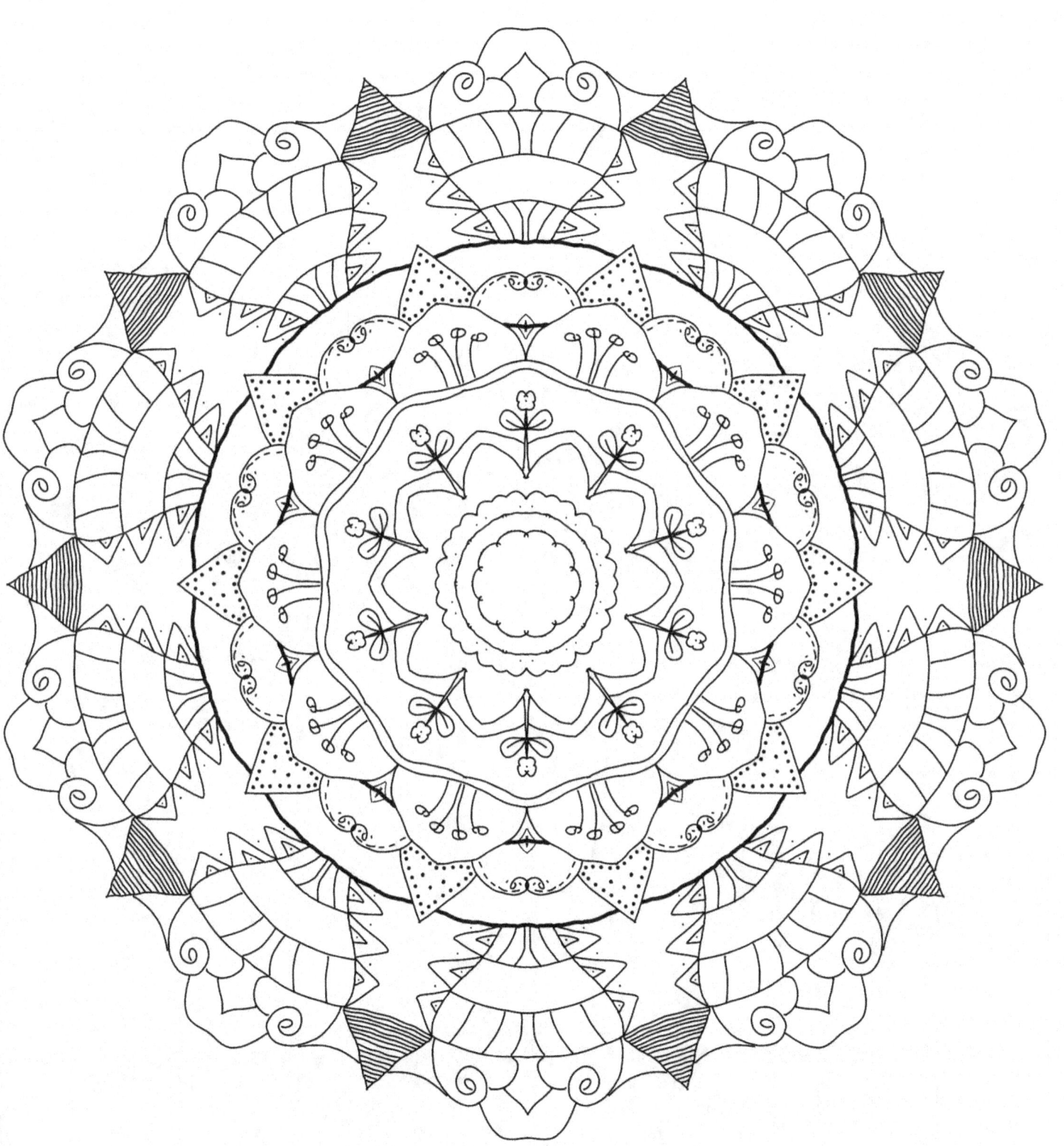

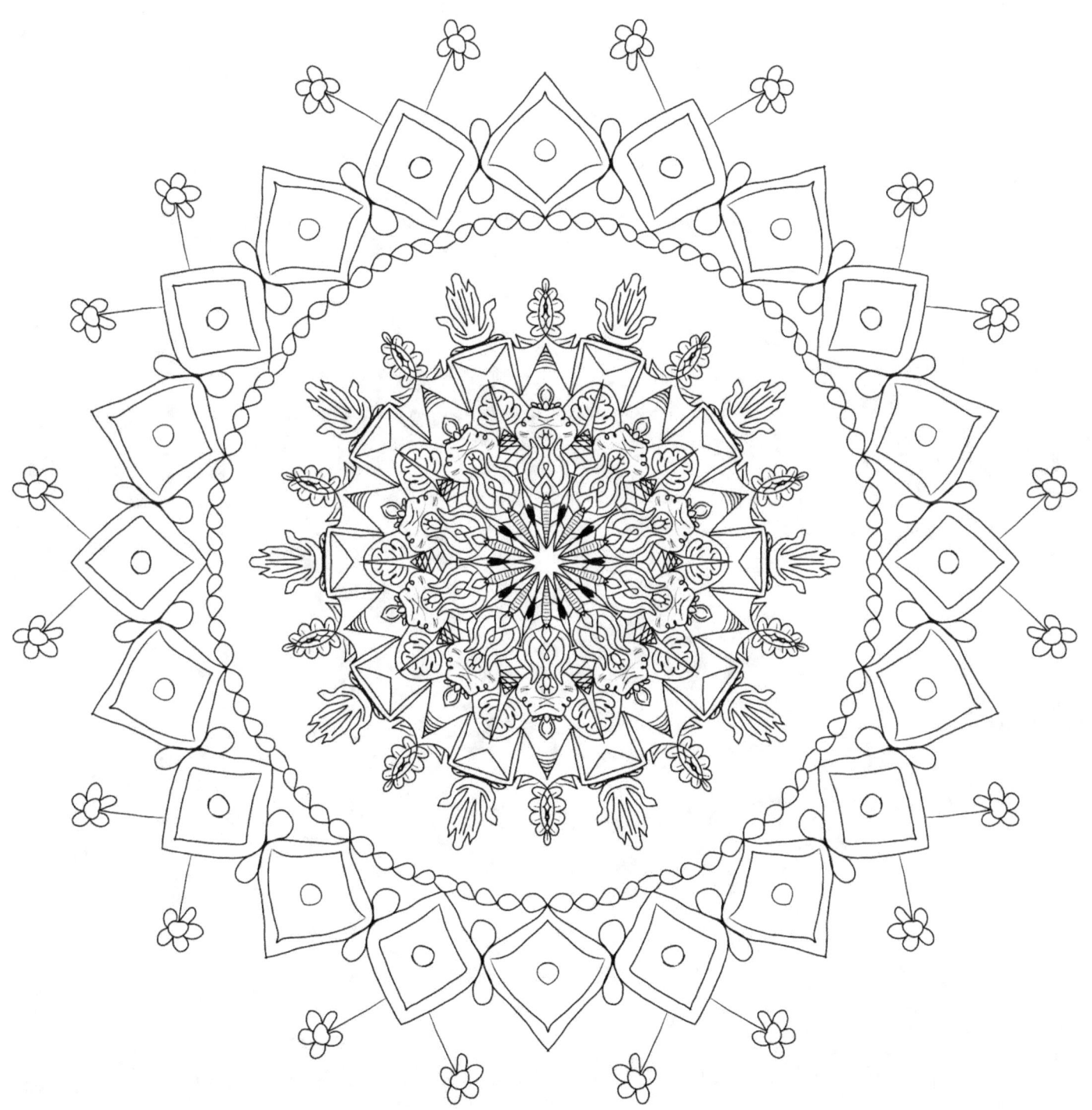

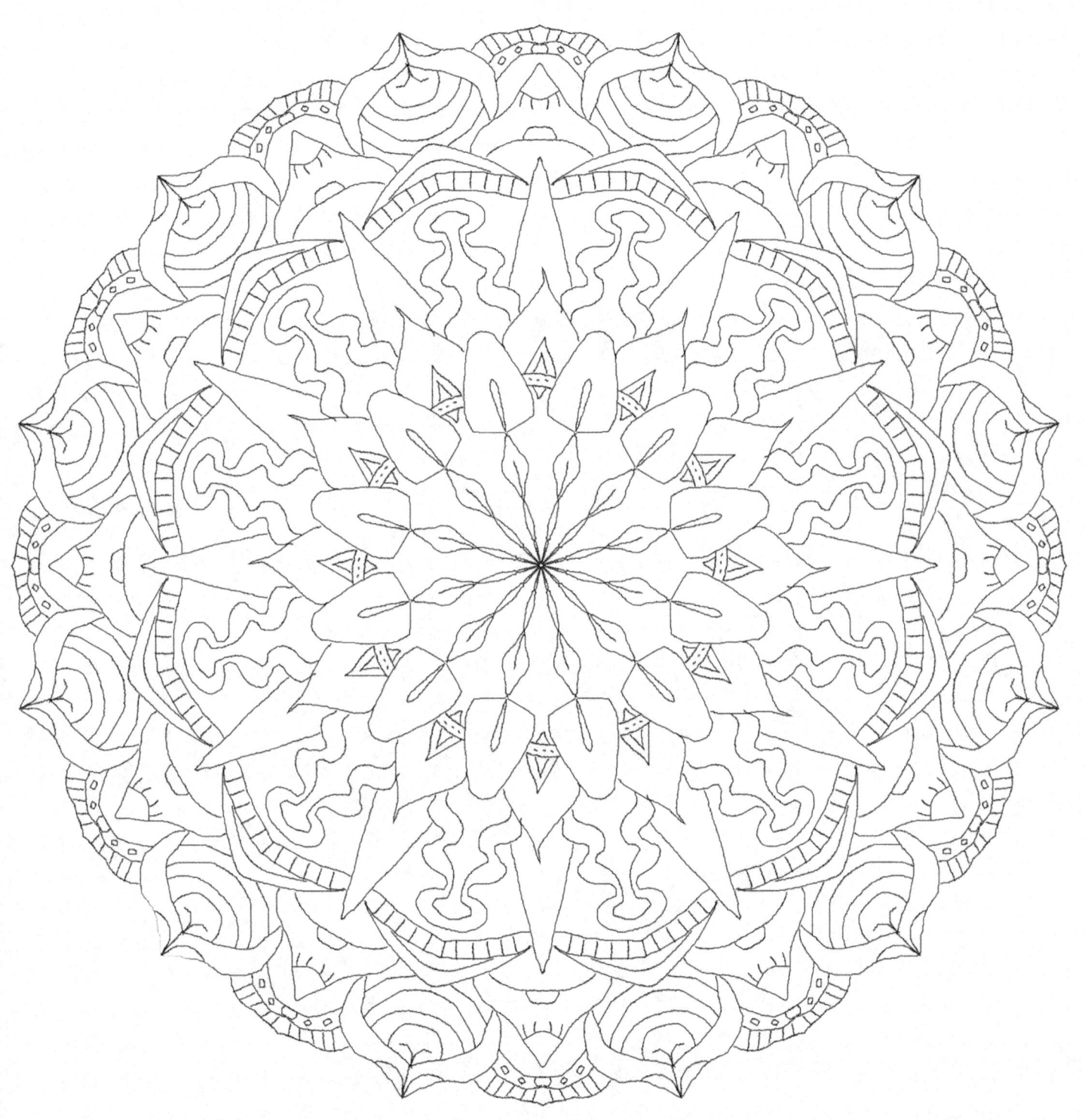

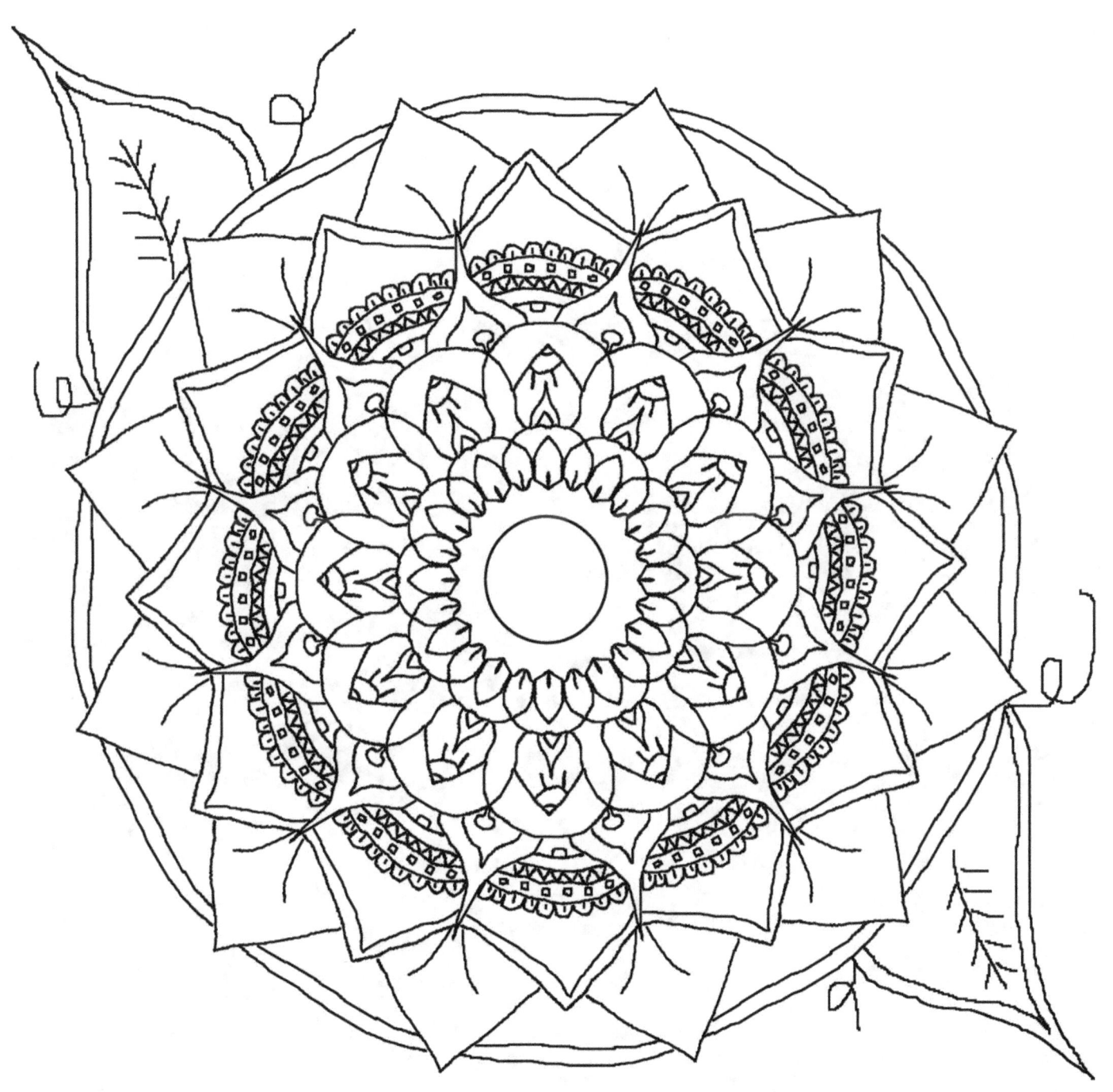

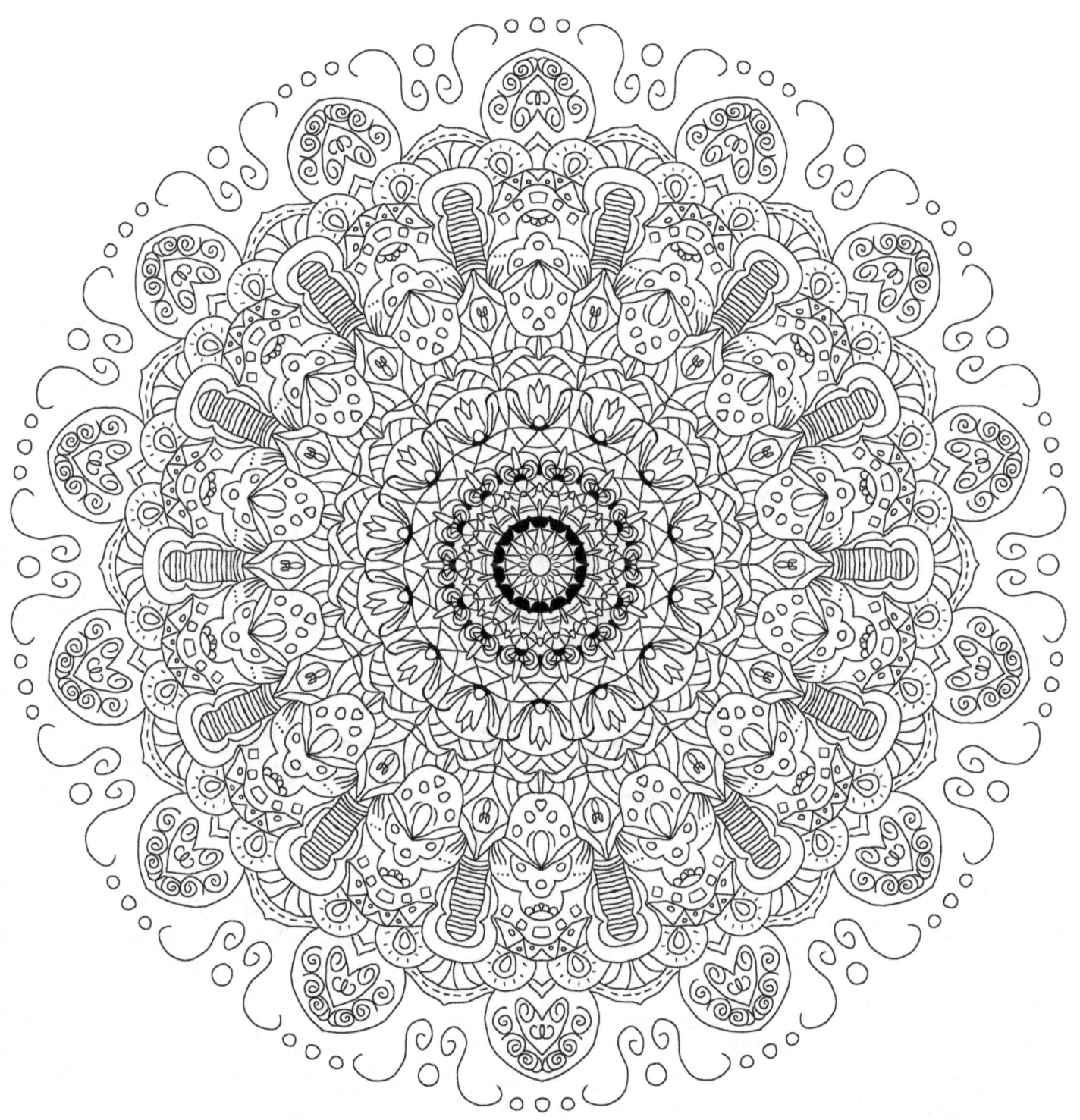

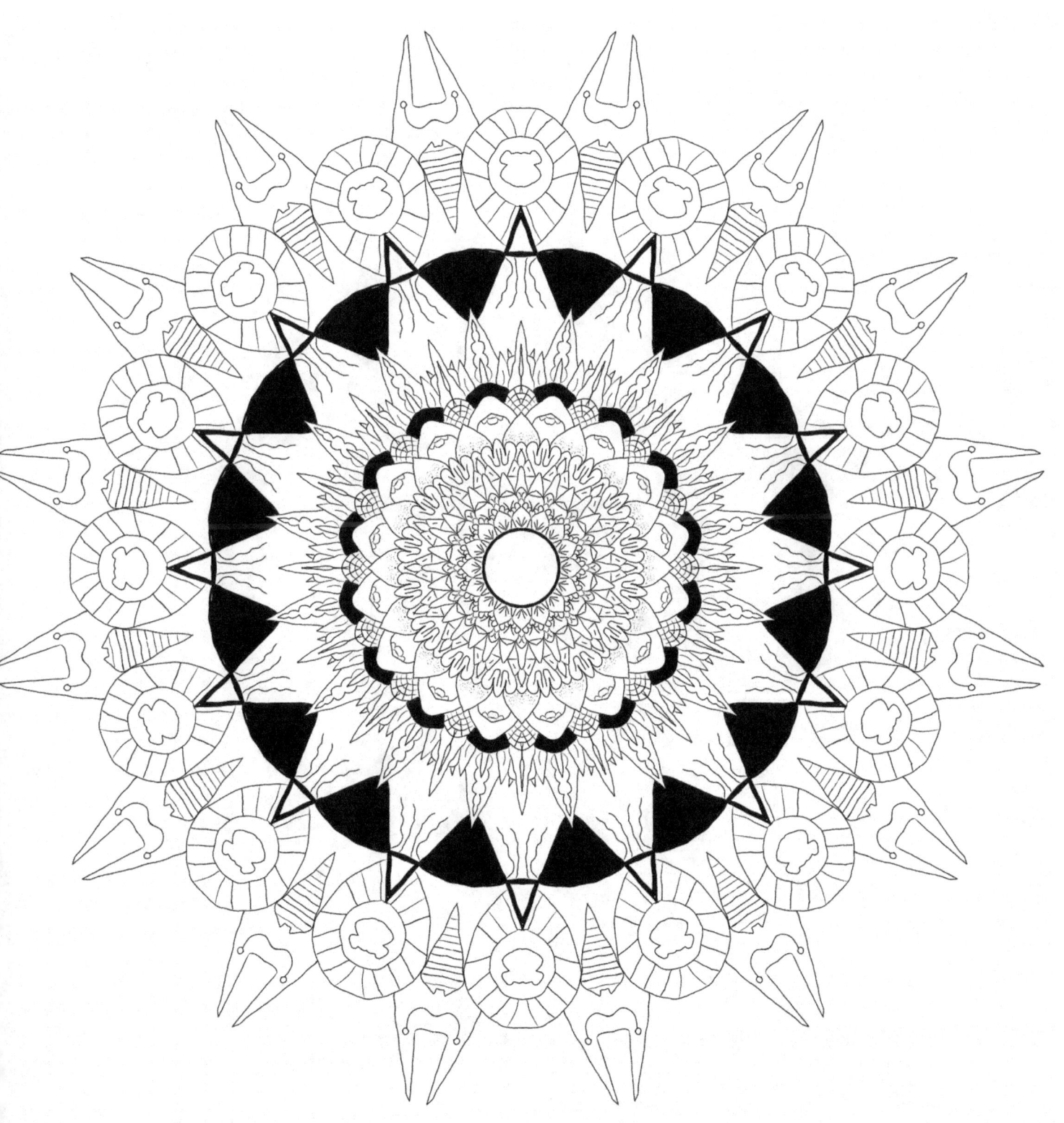

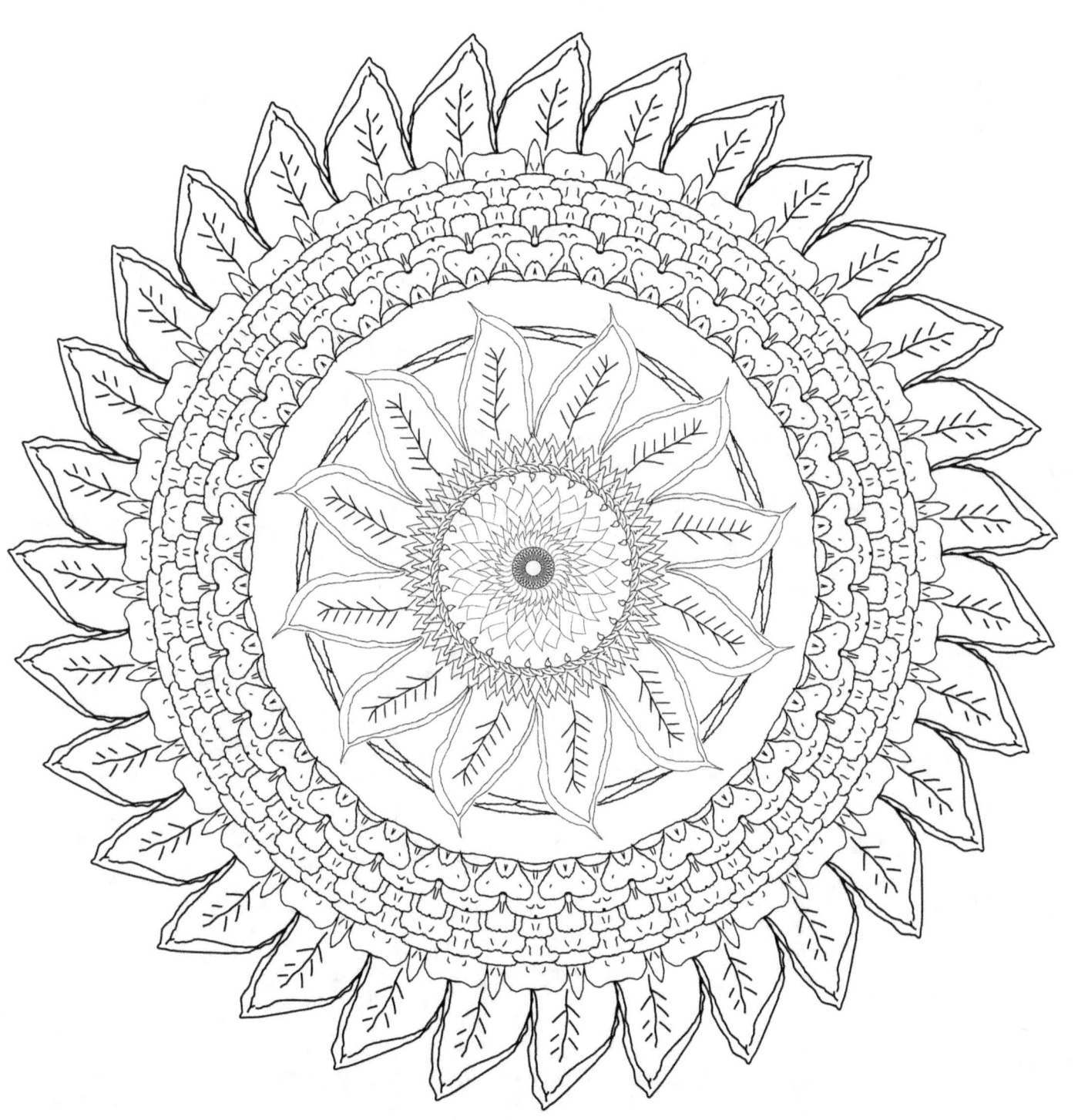

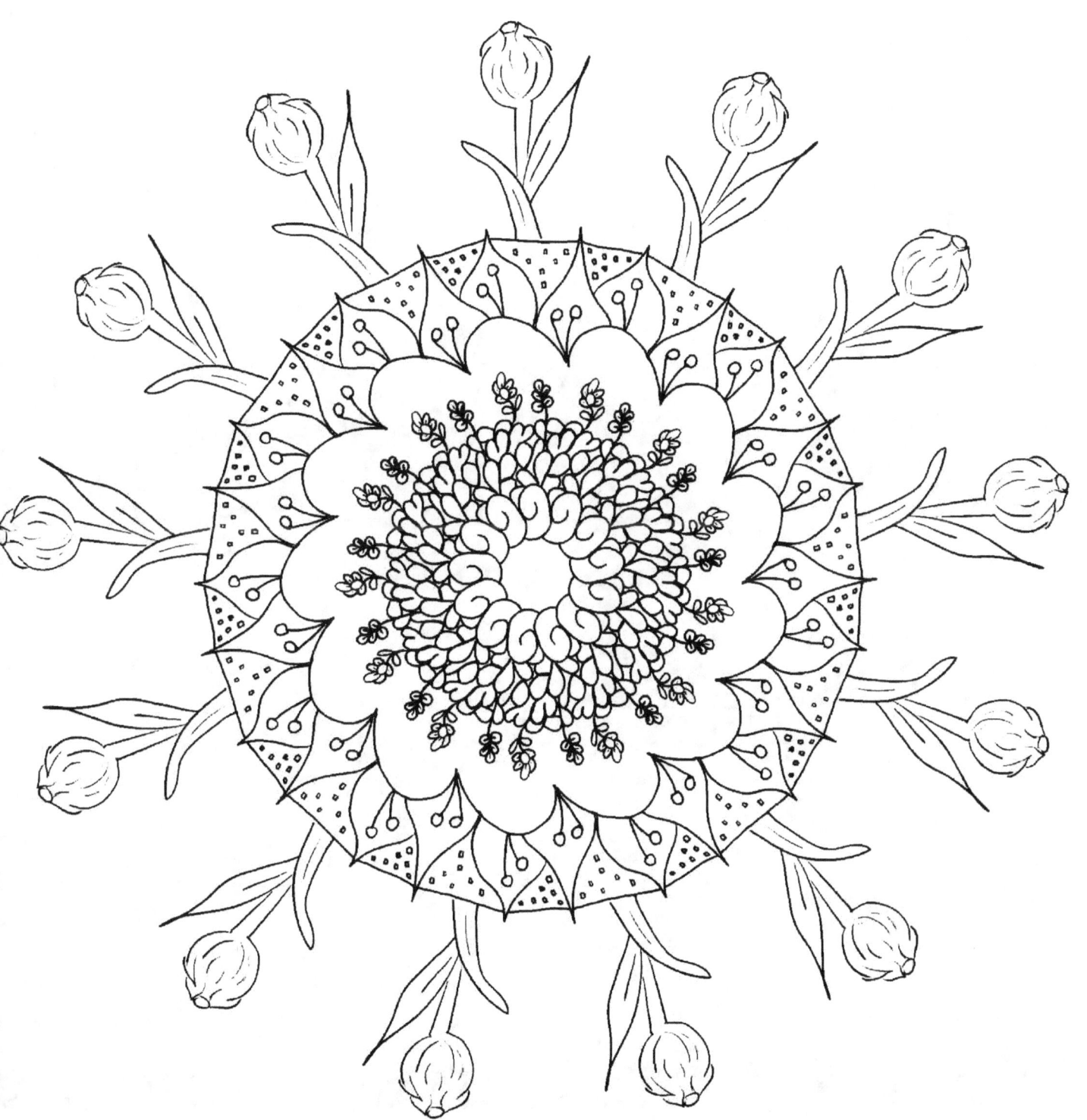

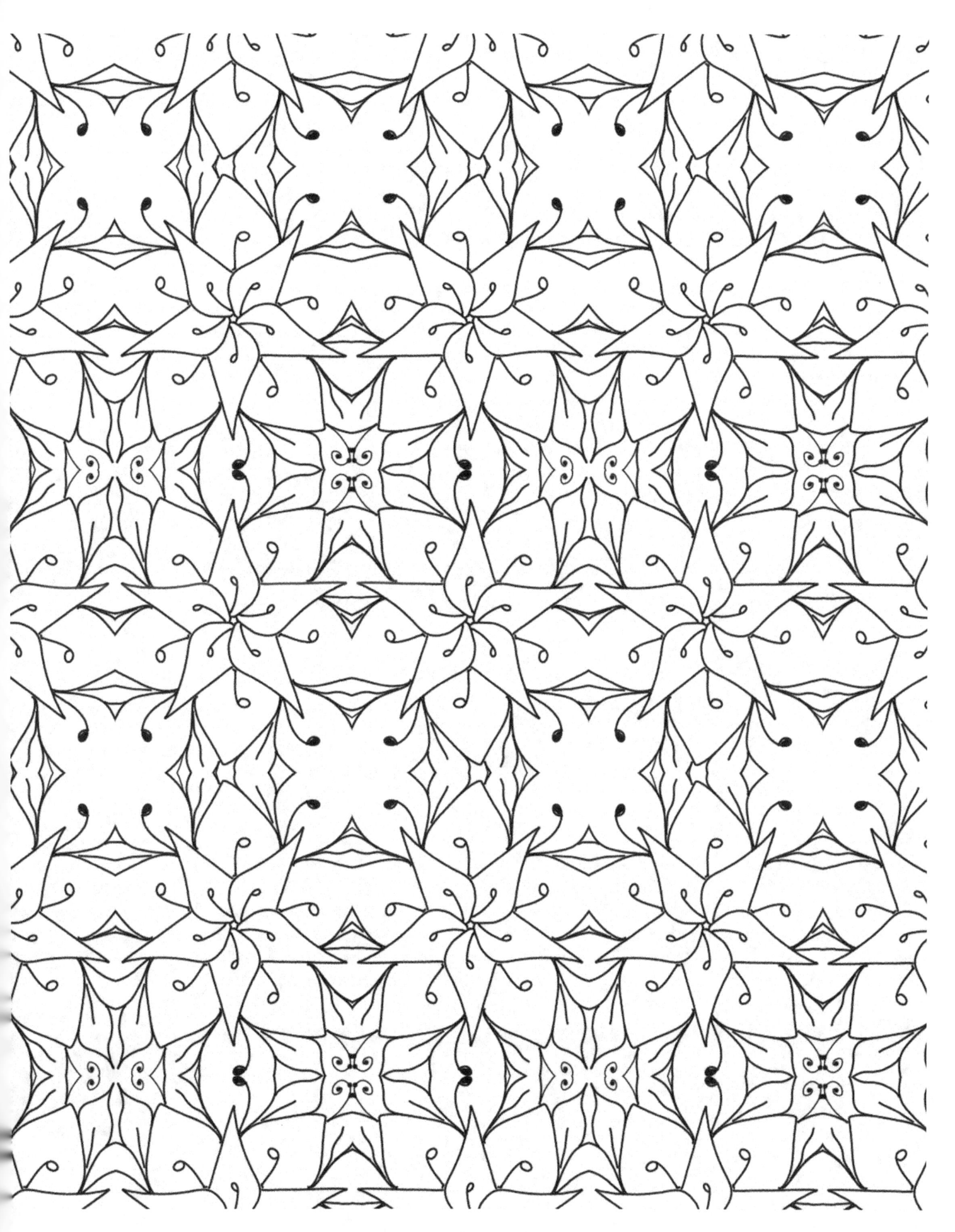

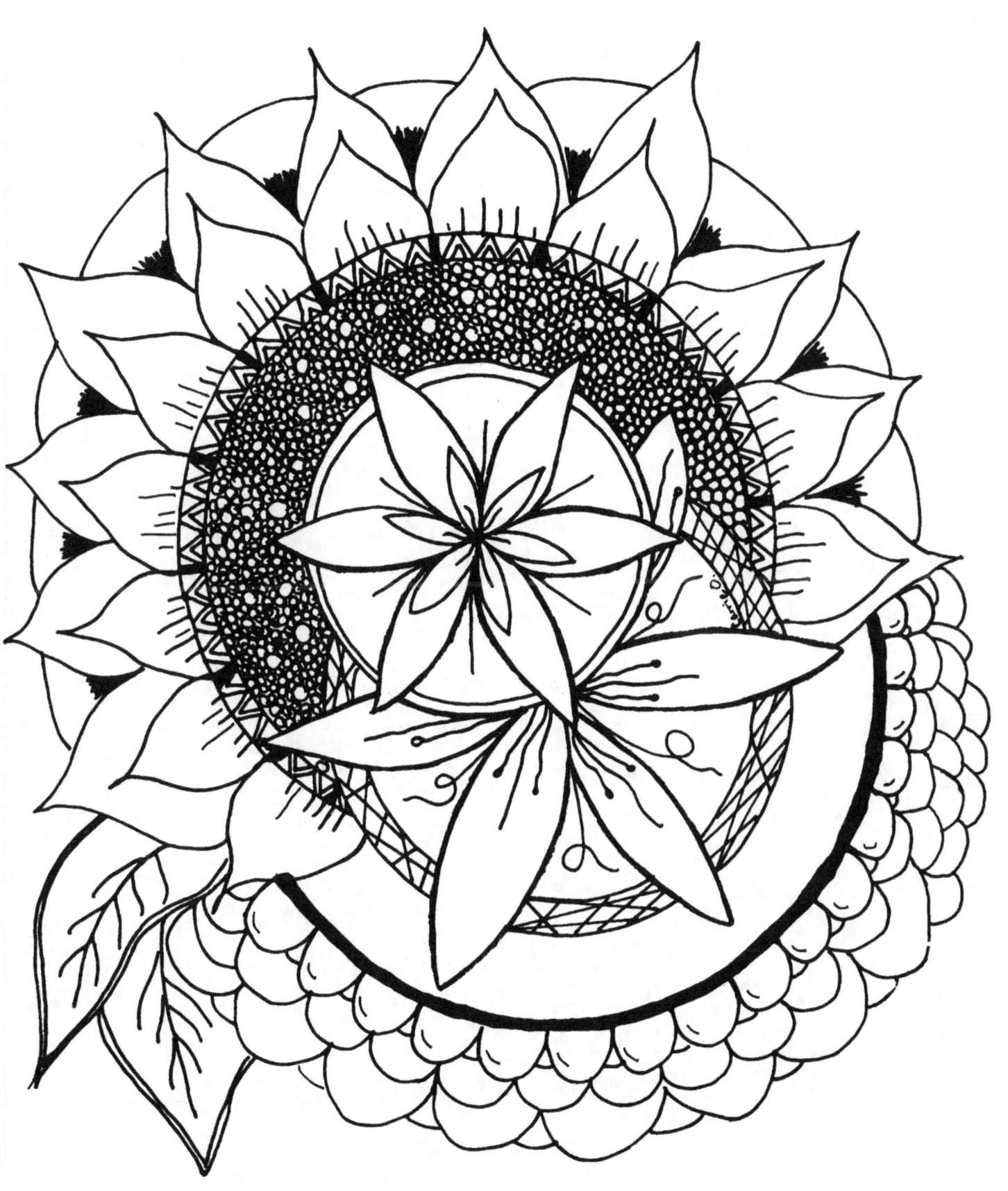

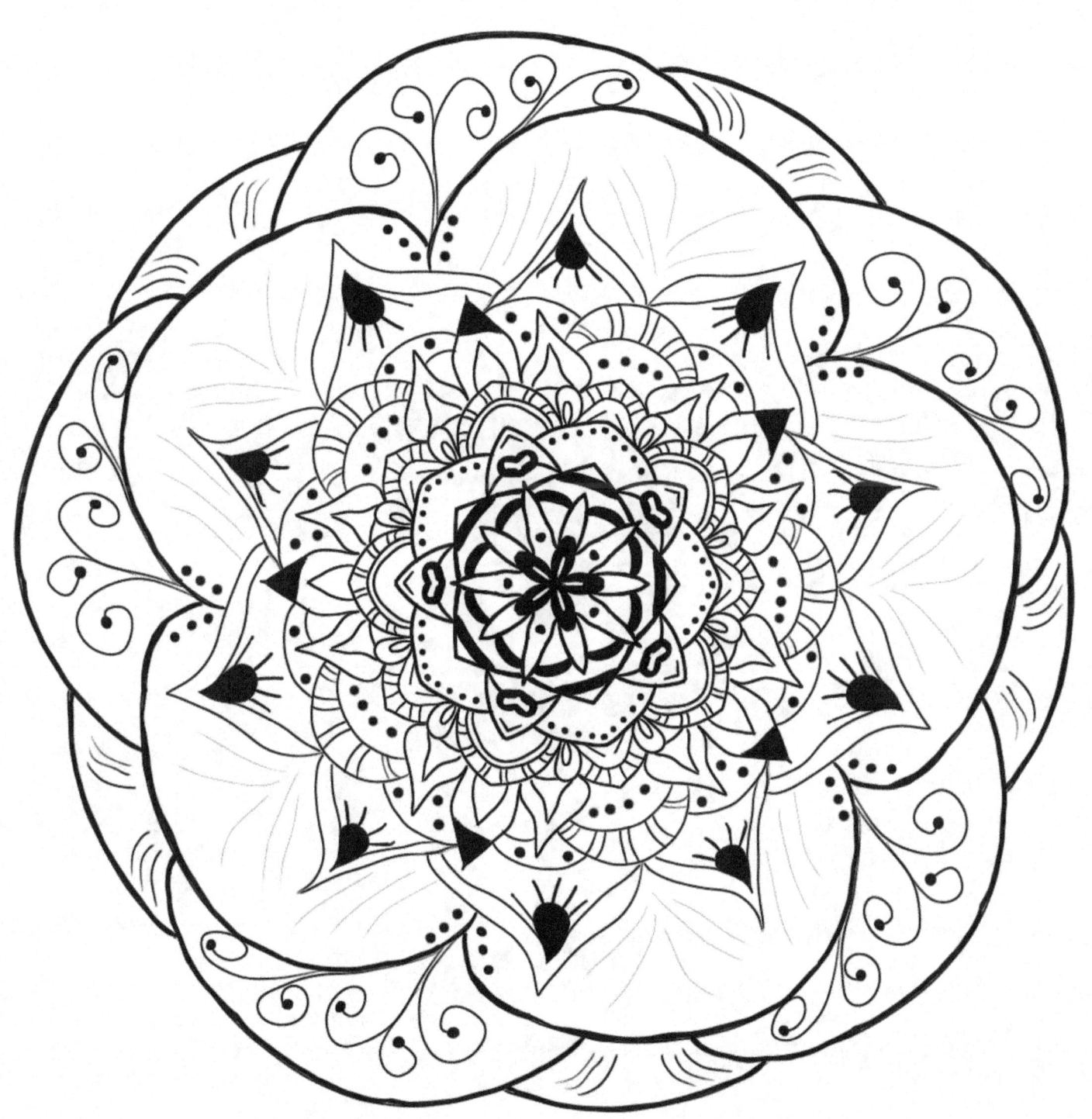

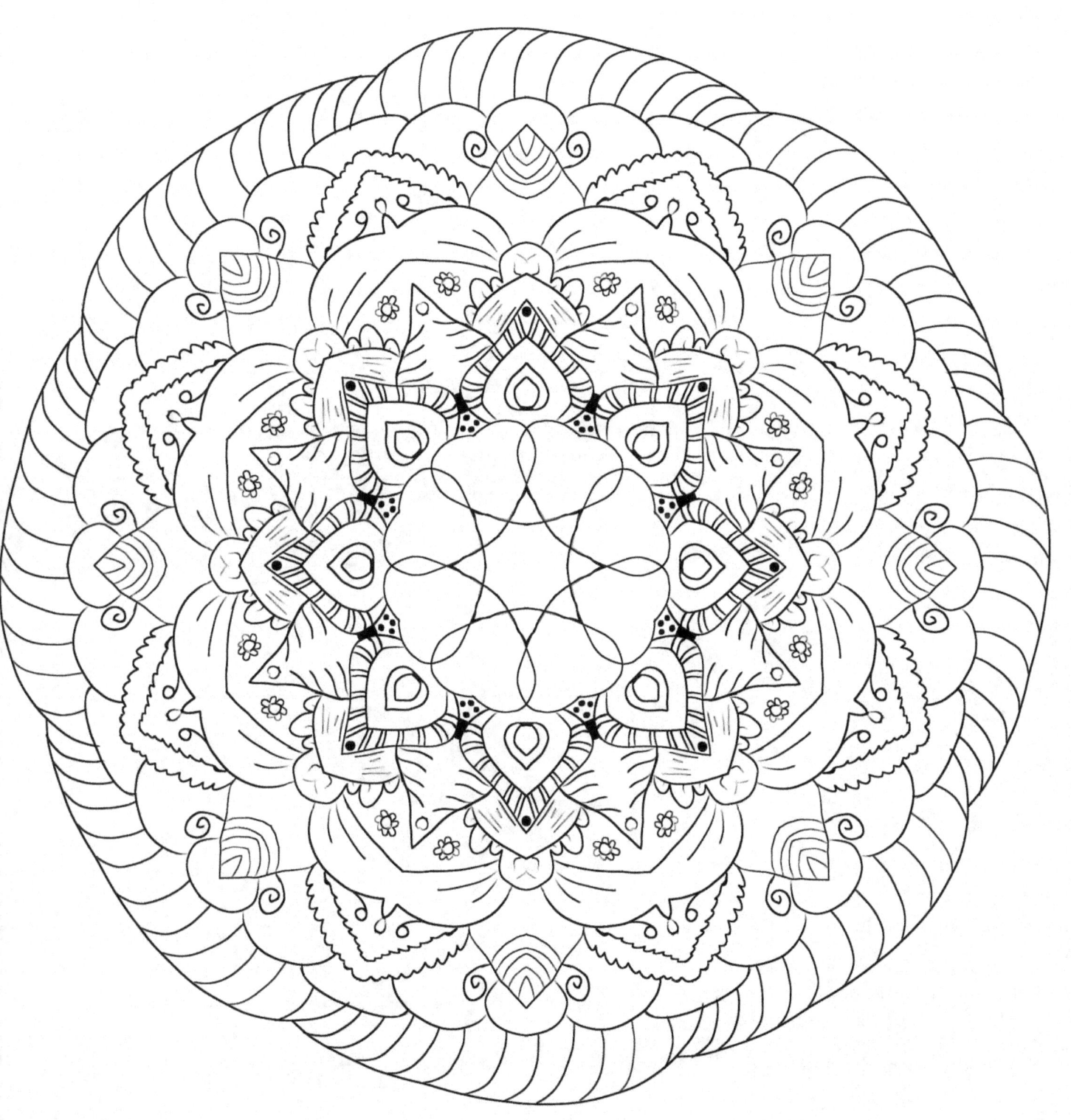

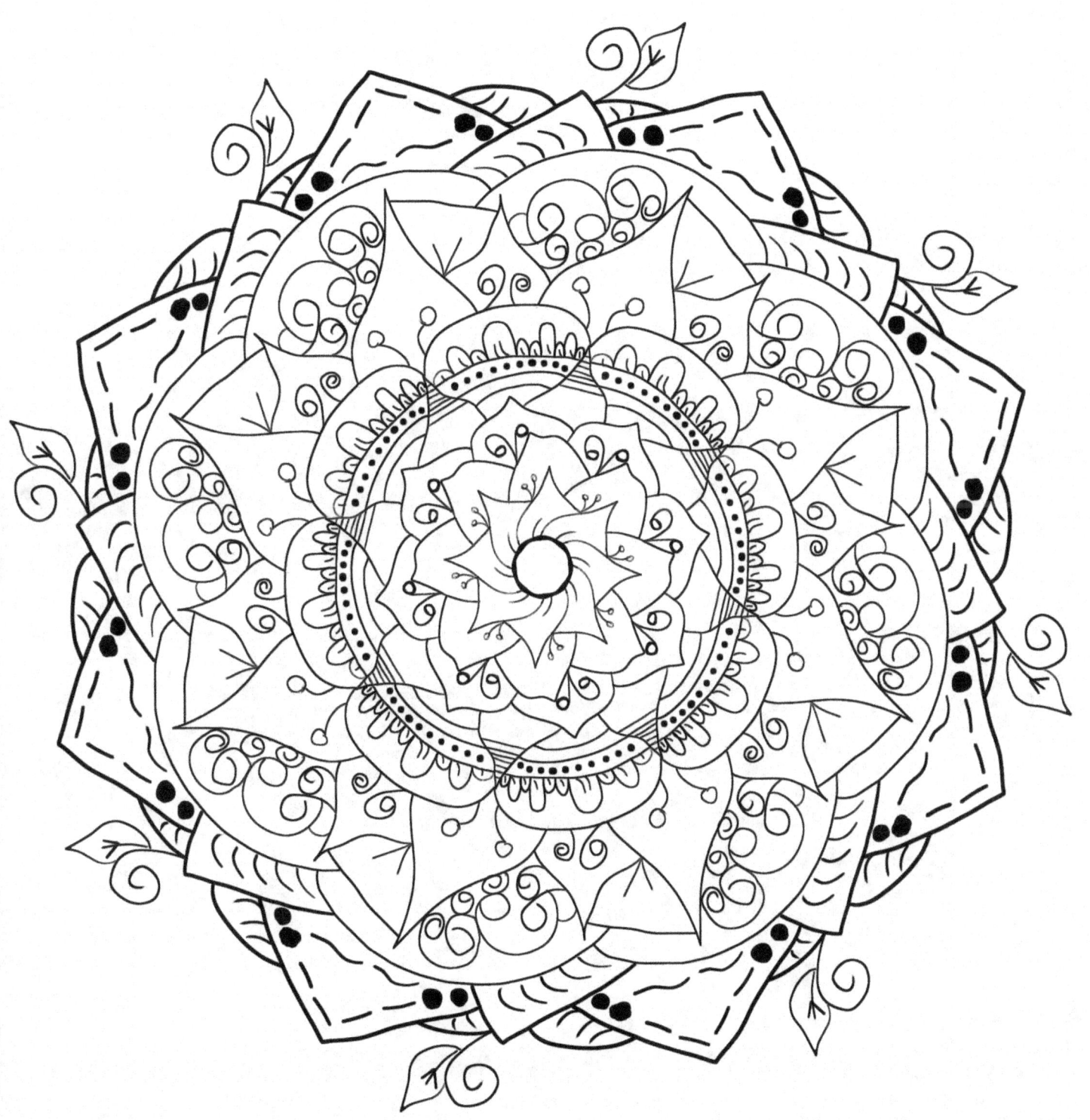

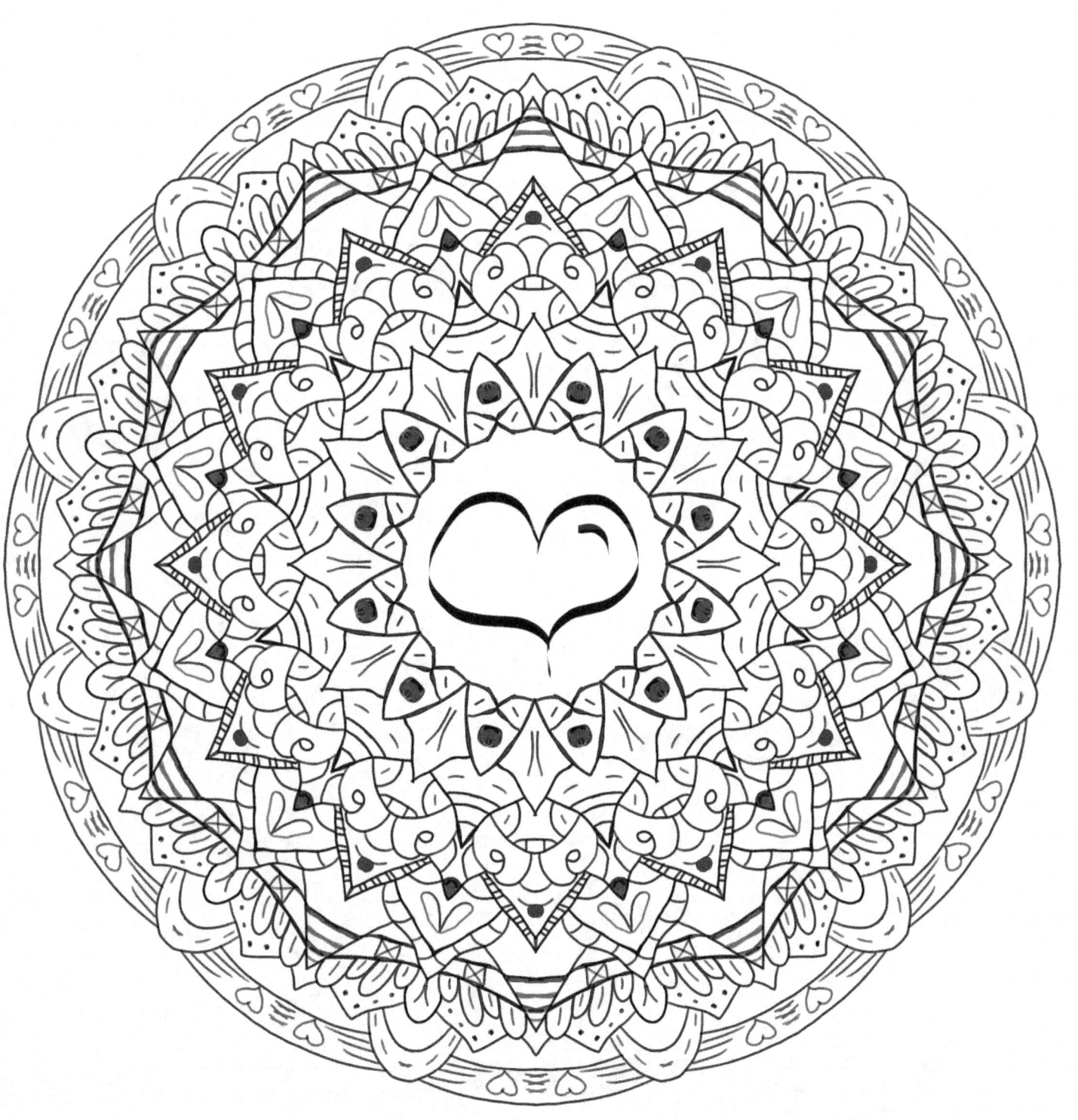

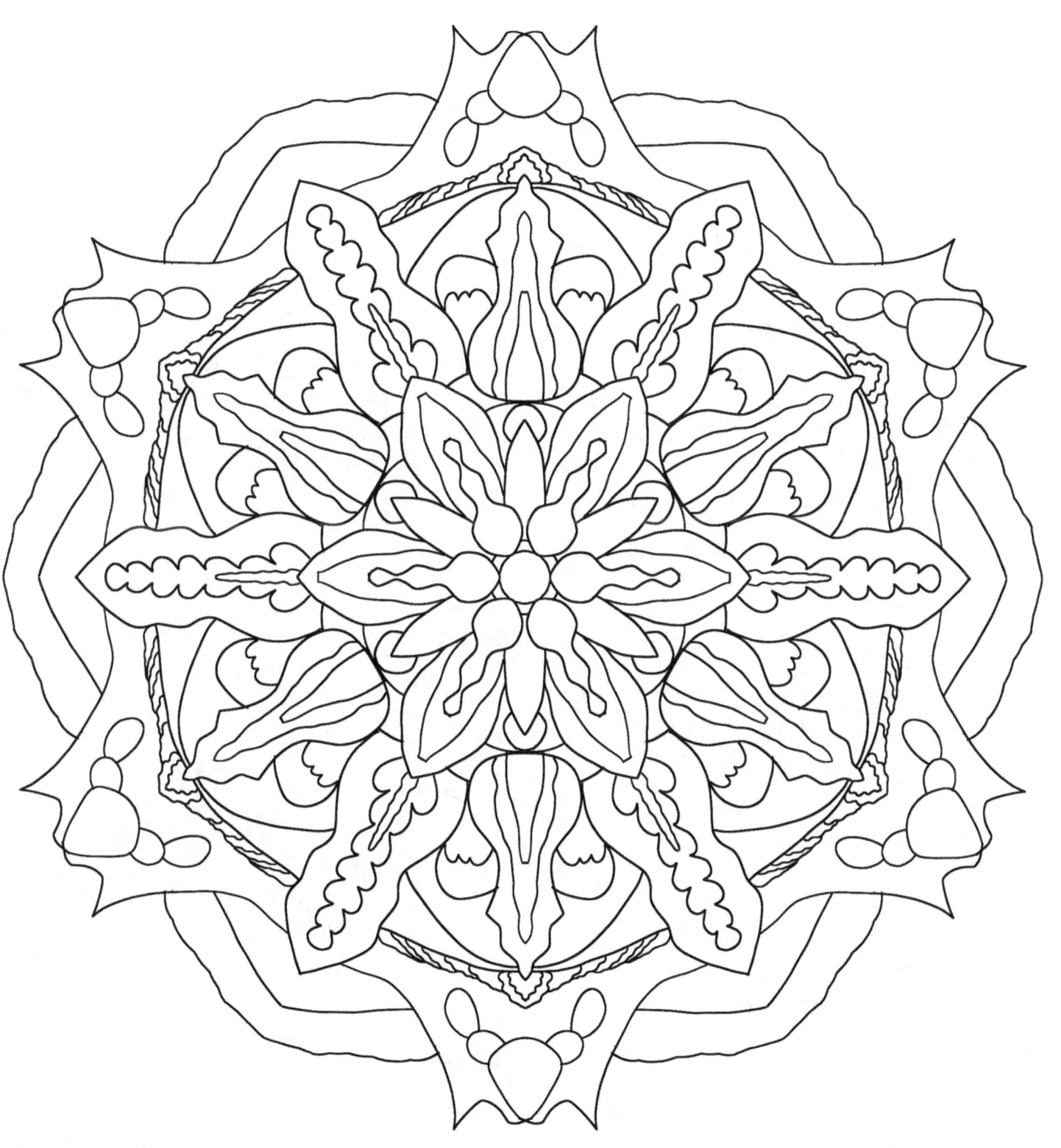

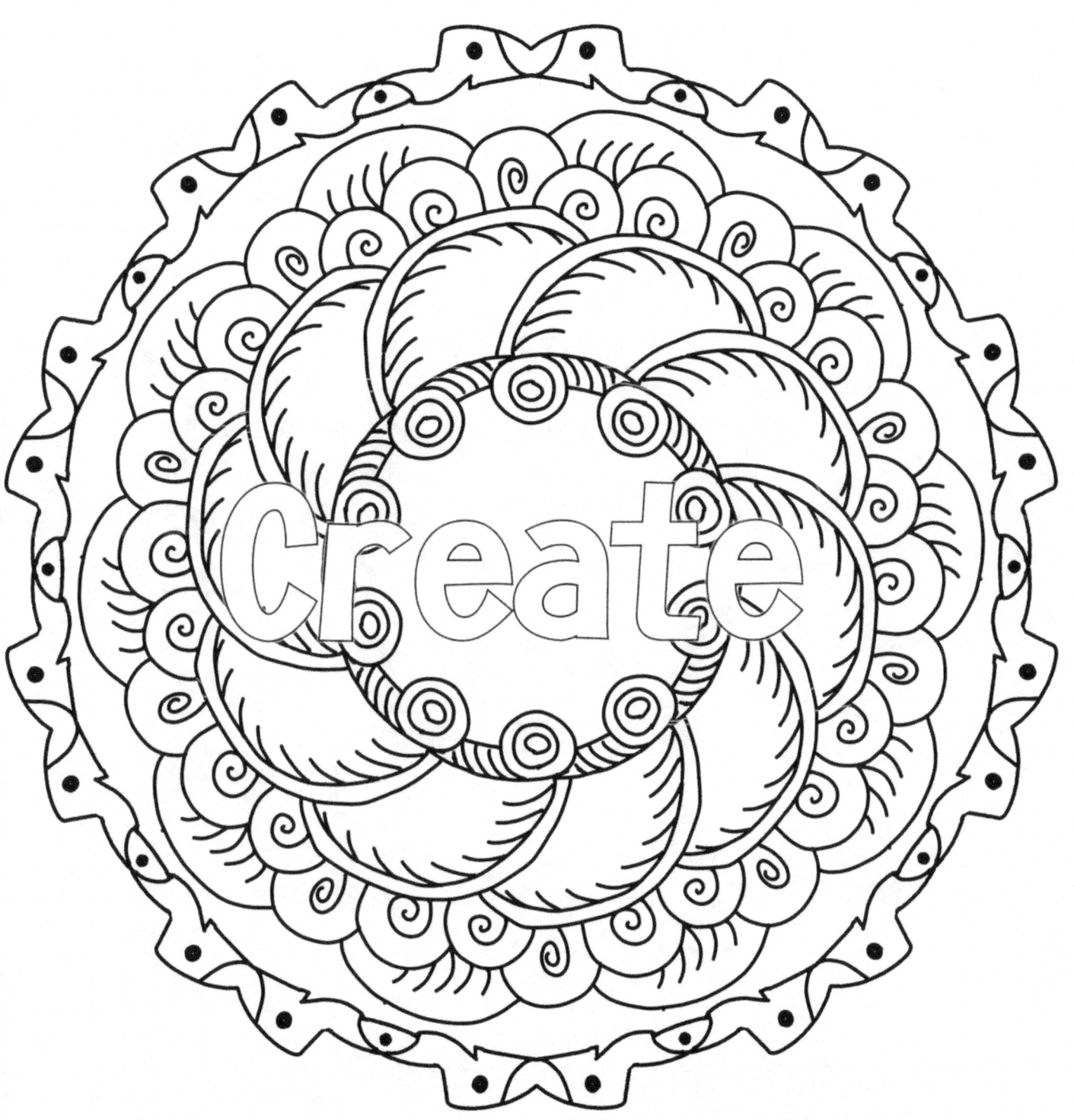

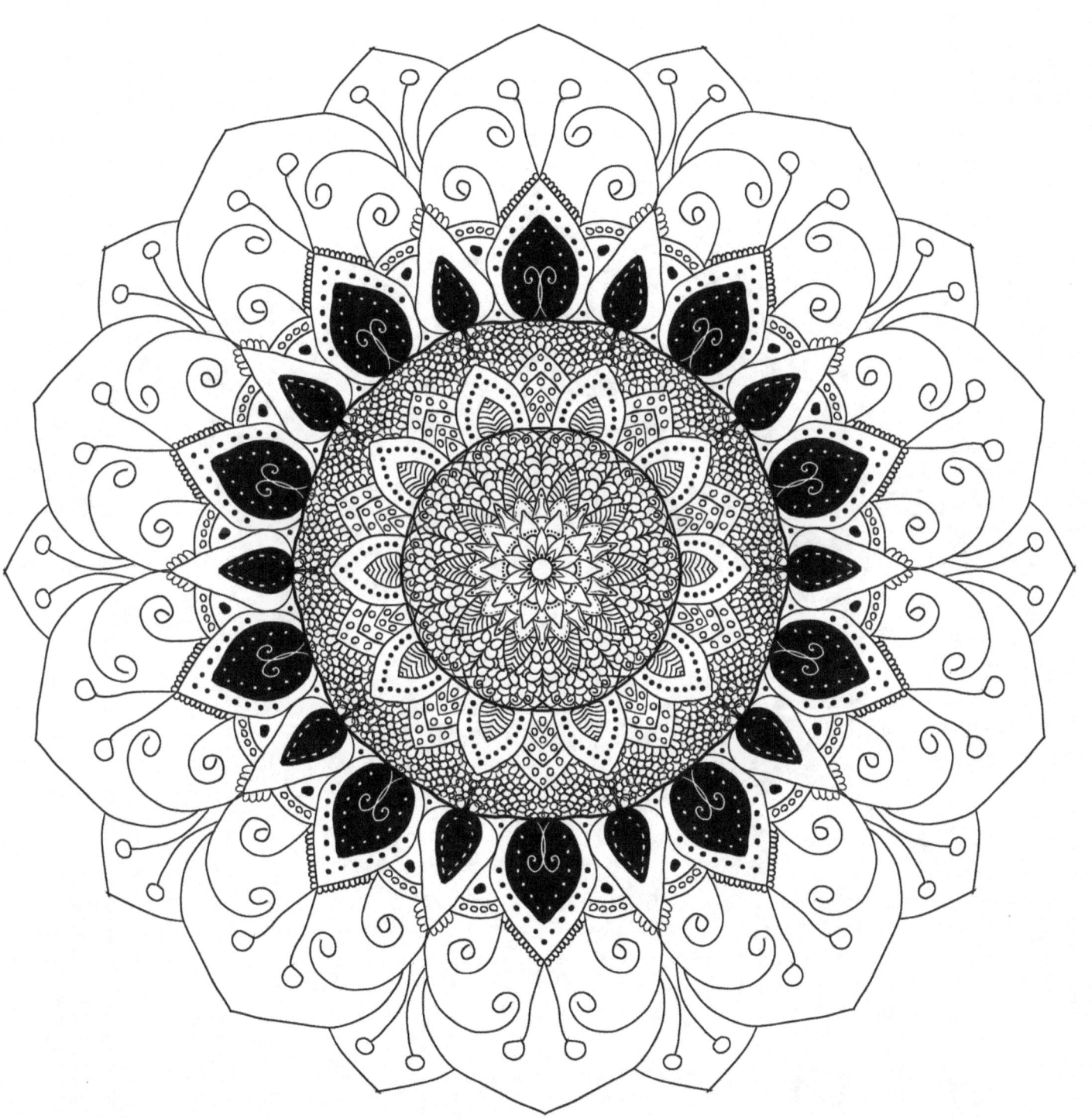

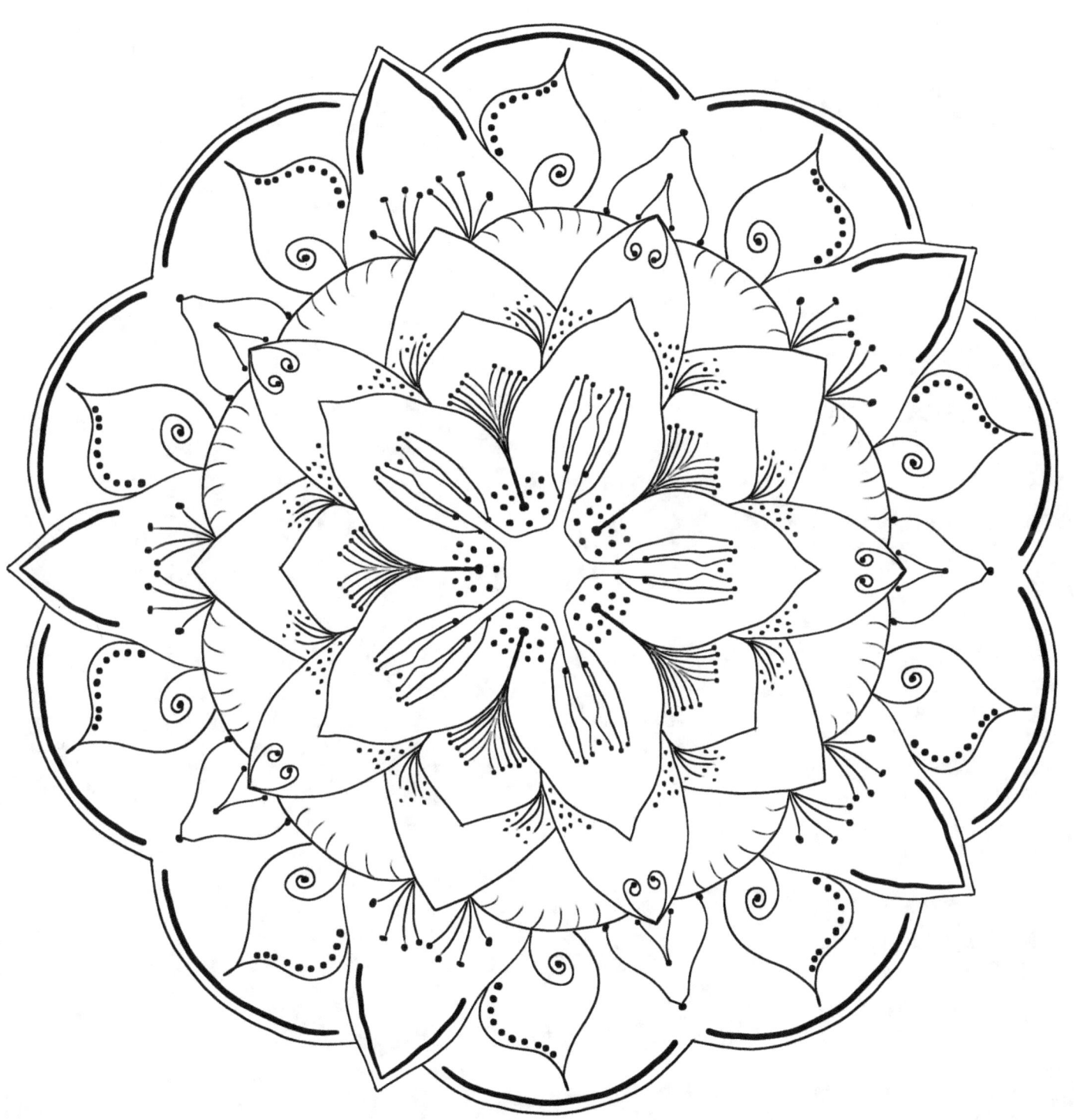

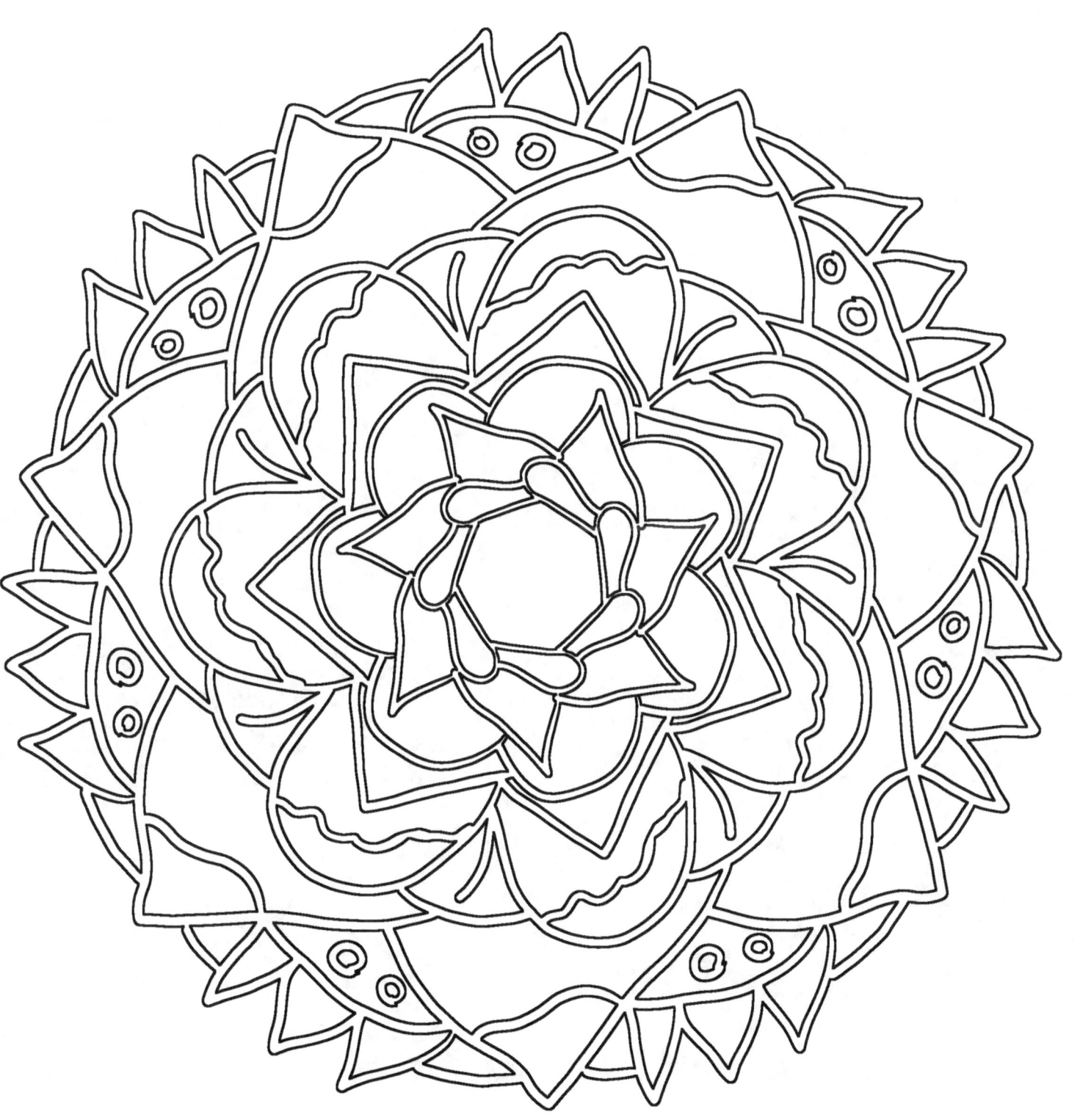

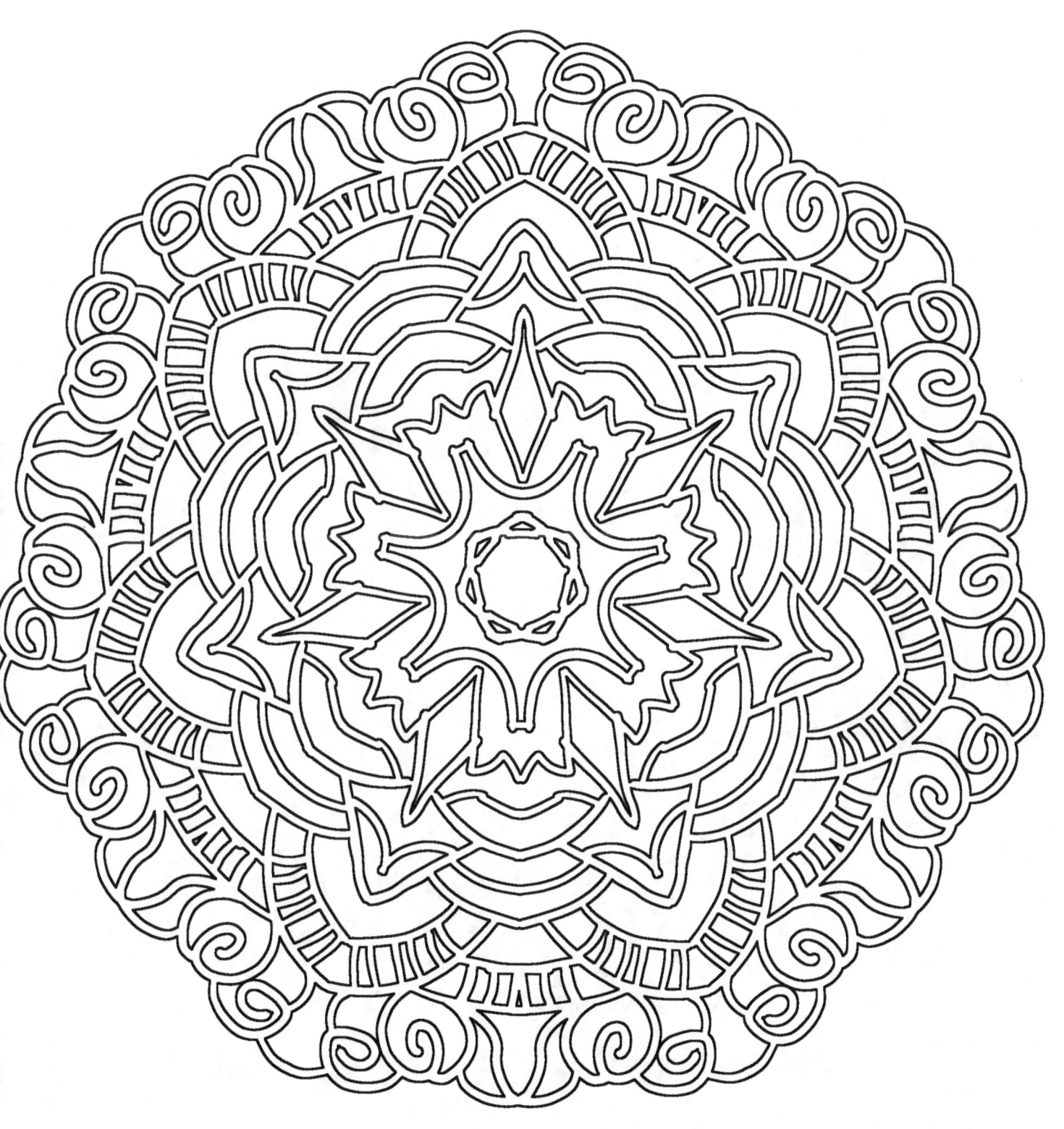

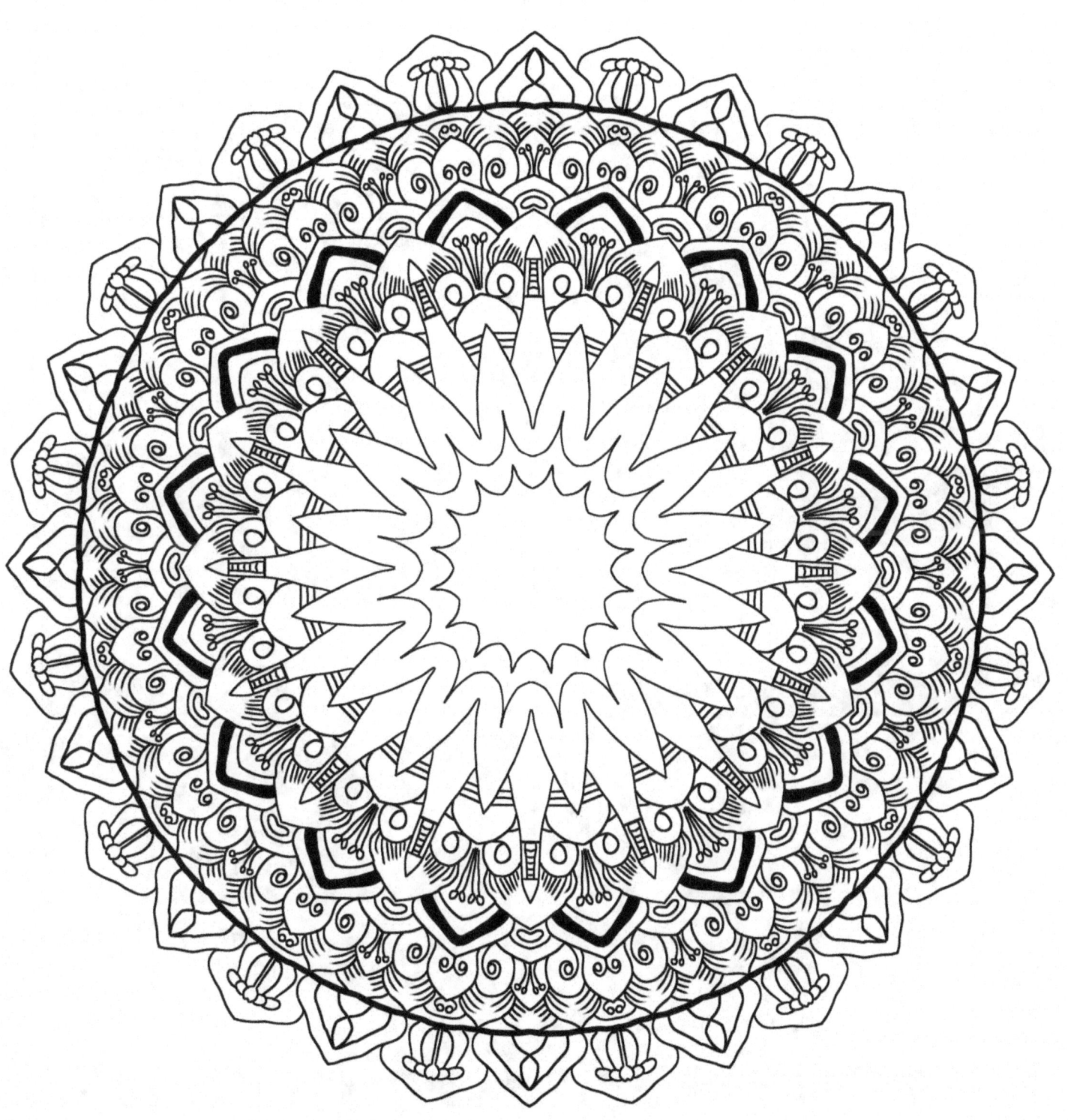

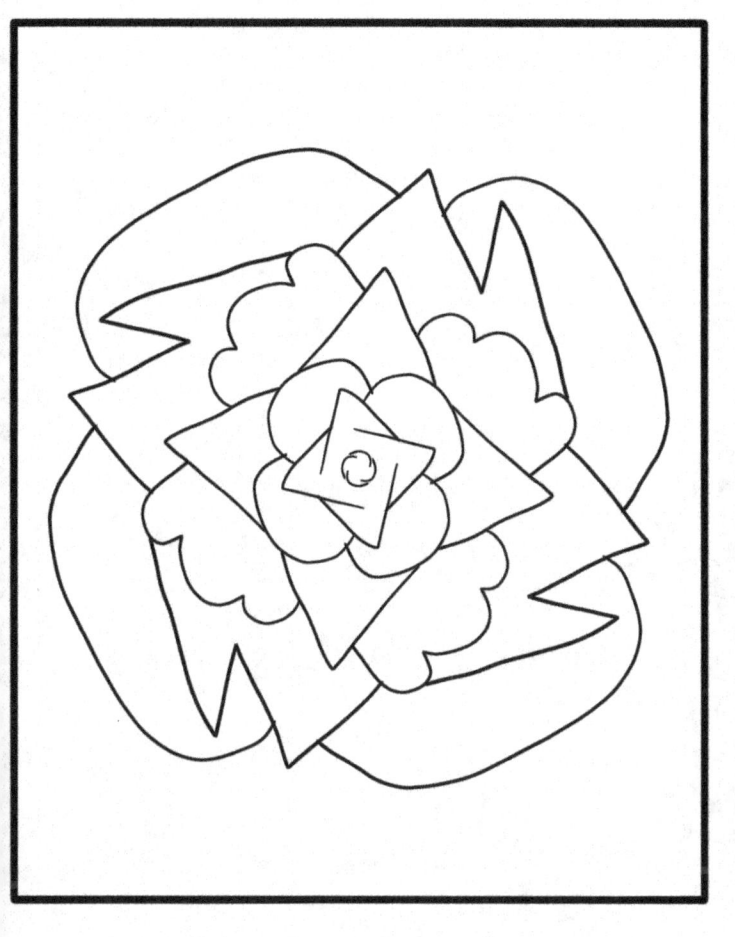
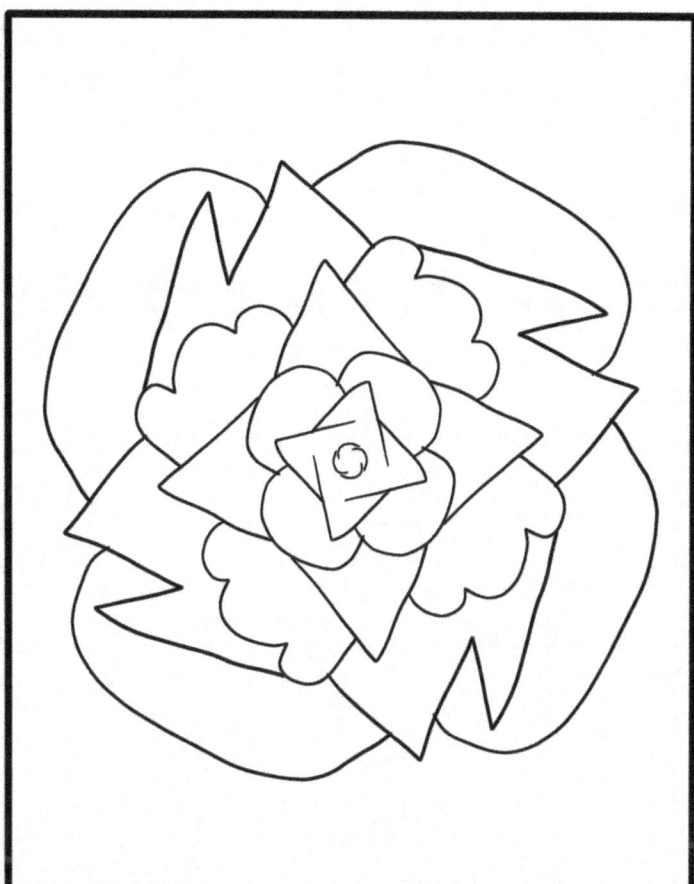
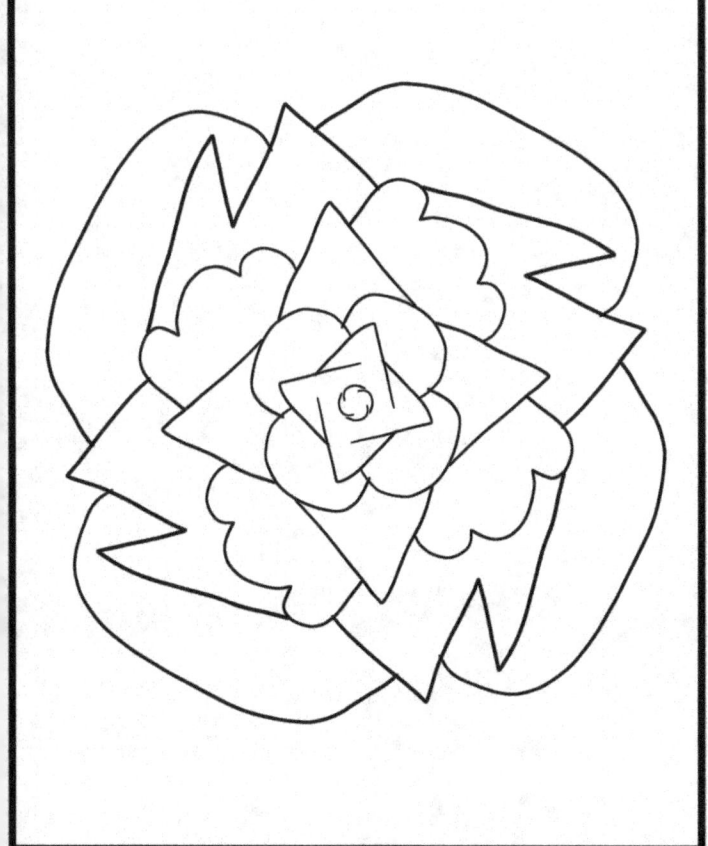
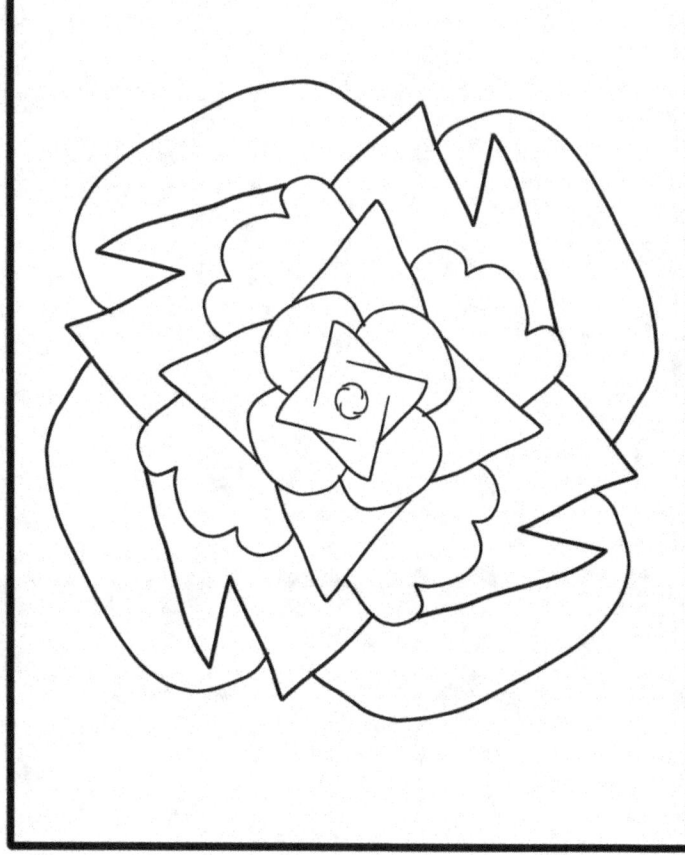

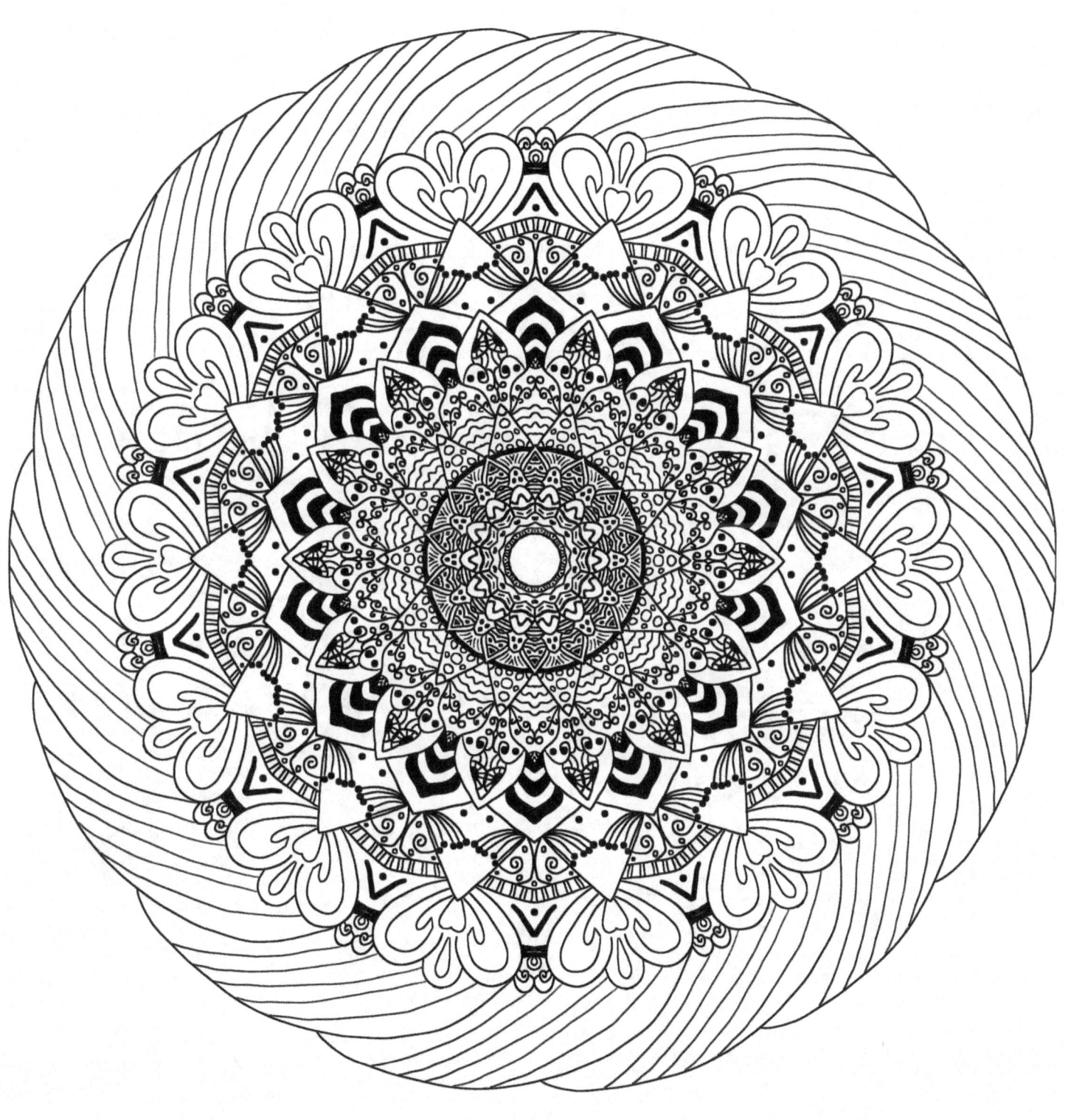

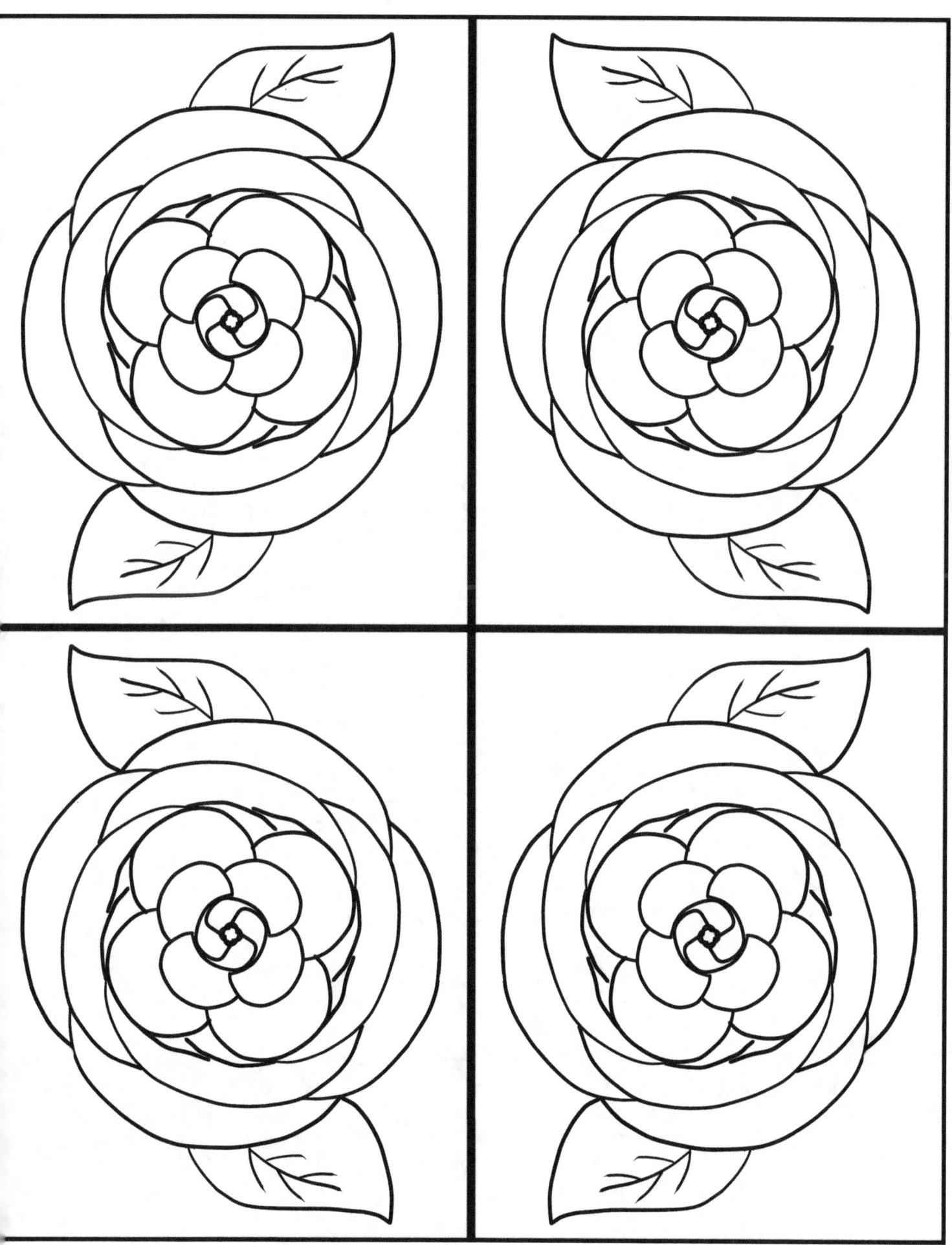

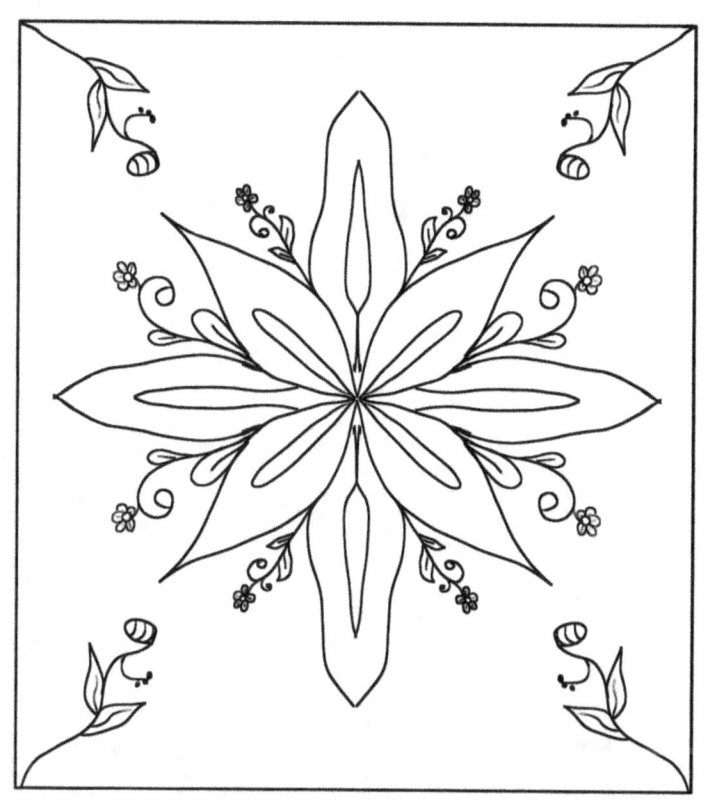
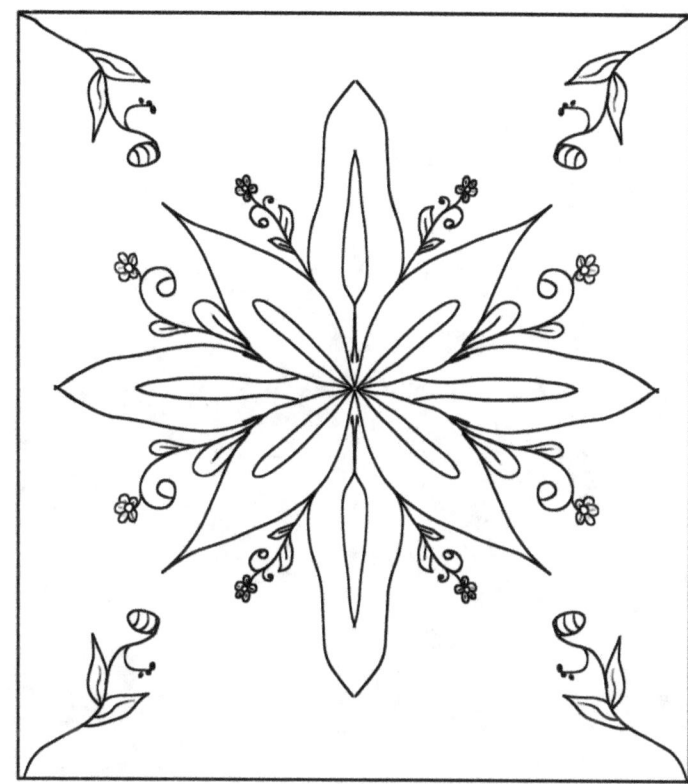
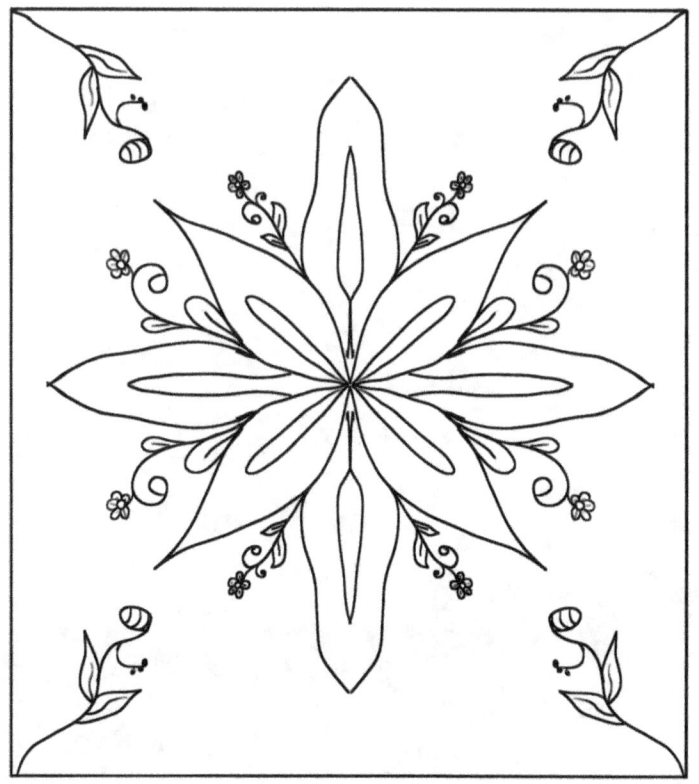

Please share your finished work with me
Facebook.com/carrieosburndesigns

-Scrap Paper-

Please share your finished work with me
Facebook.com/carrieosburndesigns

-Scrap Paper-